Things
They
Didn't
Teach Me
in
Worship Leading
School

Compiled
and edited by

TOM KRAEUTER

Emerald
Books

P.O. Box 635
Lynnwood, Washington 98046

Training Resources • Hillsboro, Missouri

Things They Didn't Teach Me in Worship Leading School
© 1995 Training Resources, Inc.
8929 Old LeMay Ferry Road
Hillsboro, MO 63050
(314) 789-4522

ISBN 1-883002-31-1

Published by Emerald Books
P.O. Box 635
Lynnwood, Washington 98046

Printed in the U.S.A.

Dedication

We, the writers of this book, humbly dedicate these stories of our experiences to the thousands of men and women around the world who regularly lead worship in a local church. Thank you for your dedicated "front-lines" ministry. We pray that you will glean both comfort and wisdom from our experiences.

Thanks to:

- Those who prodded me over the years to compile a book such as this.

- Those who diligently prayed for each step of this book—you played a greater role than you now realize!
- Pam Caldwell for typing most of the stories—I don't know of anyone else who could have done it so quickly!
- The word-processing class at Christian Outreach School, Hillsboro, Missouri, for diligently typing a portion of this manuscript—great job!
- Jennifer Brody for final copy editing—tremendous work, as usual!
- My family for allowing me to take the many hundreds of hours necessary to complete this project—you guys are the best!

Contents

Introduction

This book is entitled *Things They Didn't Teach Me In Worship Leading School*. The fact is, however, most people who are worship leaders (a trendy title for minister of music) did not go to school to learn the ropes. Often they are gifted musicians who are thrust into music ministry because of their musical abilities. If this describes you, the prayer of all of us involved in this book is that through this publication you will pick up at least a few tidbits of worthwhile ideas from experienced folks.

Some of the stories will make you laugh; others might make you cry. Some offer specific practical help for music ministers while others address life issues. All of them will encourage you to continue on, wholeheartedly in what God has called you to do.

Keep pressing on and pressing in to Him. He that began the good work in you will be faithful to complete it (Philippians 1:6).

Danny Daniels

Danny Daniels is a veteran of Christian music ana ministry, starting in the "Jesus Movement" in the early '70s and continuing as a founding member of the Maranatha! Music group, "Bethlehem." Danny has also served as a staff pastor and worship leader at Vineyard fellowships in California and Colorado, and has traveled the U.S. and abroad as a worship leader and conference speaker for Vineyard Ministries International.

In 1991, Danny returned to full-time music and teaching ministry, conducting conferences and performing concerts, as well as continuing to write and record new songs. Danny and his family attend the Vineyard in Aurora, Colorado, where Danny leads worship.

Danny and his wife, Cher, and their three daughters live in Arvada, Colorado.

Worship Measles

A new Bible study was going to start in the home of some of our friends. We lived just down the street, so we were looking forward to attending. After all, it would be a pleasure to be able to walk to any kind of church function, especially in Southern California where you drive everywhere!

A week or two before the study was to begin, the teacher asked me if I would lead worship. I had only been a believer for about three years, but I had been involved in music professionally for fifteen years, in the studio and on stage. I knew the songs, mostly choruses in those days, were not really musically challenging, so I agreed to lead worship.

After picking out six or eight of the songs that I enjoyed singing at our church, I went through them to make sure I knew the chord progressions. I "rehearsed for the gig," as I had learned to do for years. Having prepared myself and the material in the best way I knew, I felt ready to lead worship. In fact, I felt very confident that I could do a good job because I had been rehearsing several hours every day with a new band at the time.

The night arrived. The people arrived. I arrived and was introduced as the worship leader of the evening. We all seemed to anticipate a good time of singing to the Lord. I began the first song. It seemed like I was the only one singing because everyone else was singing so softly. Some people were just looking around. Others looked at me like I was supposed to do something. What was going on?

We finally made it through the first song and I decided I would close my eyes and get into the songs whether anyone sang or not. Then I realized that most of the people weren't keeping tempo and their phrasing of the lyrics was terrible. Didn't anyone know how to sing with all their hearts? Why try at all if you don't give it all you've got? What was wrong with these people? How could I work with a group like this?!

About four or five songs into it, I opened my eyes. The people were singing basically the same way, but what I saw was really different than when we started. Although the singing wasn't much stronger and the phrasing was just as loose, there was something going on! Many folks had their eyes closed. Some were crying. Several had lifted their hands. They actually seemed to be enjoying this! How could that be, when it was musically so un-together?

After the last song, I went out into the back yard. I

was exhausted, frustrated, and generally miserable. What a mess! I looked up and said, "Lord, that was one of the worst experiences I've ever had, and I never want to do it again! I'll just stick to concerts and recording, and leave that to someone else. At least I know how to worship You by myself!"

I couldn't believe what God clearly said to me, "You will be doing that the rest of your life."

"Whaaaat?" I responded. "That was terrible! Those people couldn't keep time or sing together to save their souls! I don't want to do *that* ever again."

"The people were fine," said God."They even worshiped Me in spite of the fact that you don't know how to lead them yet. But you'll get better."

"*I'll* get better?" I thought. "I did the songs right! What are You talking about! Is this really You, Lord?"

Well, it really was Him. And I really didn't know how to lead worship yet. Oh, I knew the songs, the chords and melodies, I even kept time well. But I was to learn that leading worship isn't just about music. It's about worshipping God with all your heart, mind and strength, while at the same time drawing people into an experience in the Spirit. It's about helping people to be themselves before God, so they can discover how much He loves them.

God put me in situations over the next several months where I could see and experience the ministries of effective worship leaders. They were each a little different and uniquely themselves, but they all showed me that it isn't just music that makes a good time of worship singing. No matter how great the singing and no matter how tight the music, without surrender and passion for God, worship does not happen. It's kind of like measles. If you've got'em, then someone can catch'em. But if you don't, no one ever will! I'm still learning twenty years later that a worship leader must be a worshipper first, and then others may be able to come into that dimension of worship that must be caught, not taught. My goal now? Give everybody worship measles.

A First-Class, Third-World Lesson

While on a trip to South Africa with a team from California, we attended a Sunday morning worship service at a Zulu church. We arrived about 9 a.m. and were met by the pastor in a side room. He told us that the service had begun at 8, but we were welcome to come in and join in the singing of worship songs still in progress. Most of us were used to singing worship songs for 20-30 minutes in Sunday morning services, so we were interested in what it was like for a congregation to worship in song for what was to us much longer than "normal."

The congregation was singing very intensely, with a

lot of clapping and many raised hands. We entered through a side door, and most of us sat in the back of the room. The first thing I noticed was that every person I could see was singing with all their heart. I could see no one who was looking around, being silent, or not participating. Looking at this group as a worship leader, it was striking to me that the level of commitment was so great.

Most of the songs were sung in Zulu, or as I was to find out later, Zulu and Sotho, the two primary languages which represented the members of the church. Some songs were sung in English.

Even more interesting than the large percentage of participation in singing, and songs being sung in three languages, was the way that the worship musicians were set up. Most of us spend a lot of time, energy and money to develop people, equipment and programs which will help our churches to have meaningful, consistent worship in our services.

Though I have been to several countries and have seen variations in how different churches conduct their music and worship programs, I had never seen anything like this. The only instrument on the platform was an electric piano, which was in desperate need of tuning. While that is not as uncommon as one might think, the fact that the person who led the singing and began each song was not even on the platform definitely was something that I had never seen anywhere.

At the beginning of each song, the keyboard player

would play a chord and let it ring out until the leader began to sing. Then the people would either pick up the song with the leader, or they would answer with a counter-melody or lyric. This wasn't something that was new to us, but the fact that we couldn't see the leader on stage was.

I tried to find the source of the voice through several songs. It was a female voice, full of emotion and passion. In fact, this lady was one of best singers I had ever heard! Her voice and spirit seemed to ignite the rest of the congregation each time she led out in song. One thing was certain, no one was distracted by the band or anything else on stage. (Something that can be a problem in churches in the U.S.) These folks were there to praise the Lord!

I finally found her. Sitting in the section to the right of the center aisle, about five rows from the front, was a girl who looked to be about 15 or 16 years old. Her hands were raised, her head was lifted up, and she had a glorious glow on her face. She knew where the holy place was and how to get there, and everyone followed her in! This was worship leading in its purest form.

I began to have a great time. When the songs were in English, I sang as I learned how it went. When they were in the native languages, I sang in tongues. It was really good. There was such a freedom without any performance or ego trips going on that it freed us all up to focus on Jesus completely.

I returned home having learned that we don't have to change our stage set-up or only have one keyboard on stage. I don't have to sit in the 5th row or get rid of the rest of the band. But no matter what logistical structure we have, it should be what the Holy Spirit has shown us is best for who we are. And whatever it is, we must totally abandon ourselves to worshiping and praising our Savior. From that time on, we began to experience a new freedom and release to the Lord, and He in turn poured out His love like never before. I had learned a first-class lesson from what some call "third-world" people. Love God, believe His word, and praise Him with all of your heart.

Howard Rachinski

Howard Rachinski is president and CEO of Christian Copyright Licensing, Inc. (CCLI), and founder of the Church Copyright License, which helps churches comply with the copyright law. CCLI is currently serving approximately 100,000 churches in Australia, Canada, New Zealand, the United Kingdom, the United States and South Africa.

Howard has experience as a songwriter, arranger, record producer and music sales manager and is recognized as an experienced seminar leader and contributing editor in music copyright law issues. His experience also extends to the local church arena where he was an associate pastor for seven years and a music minister for five years in one of the nation's largest churches where he directed an 80-voice choir and a 30-piece orchestra.

Howard is recognized as an enthusiastic conference speaker, specializing in the areas of praise and worship, music culture, music ministry and worship leading. Howard and his wife, Donna, live with their three children in Portland.

A Smile in My Eyes

⟨⟩⟨⟩⟨⟩

My 19-year-old daughter is currently experiencing that "struck by the lightning of love" syndrome that hits all of us sooner or later. She met her boyfriend during her first year of Bible College and, as is the case with an out-of-town college boyfriend, we get to see him in our house quite regularly for "feedings and washings."

It was during one of these visitations that I was able to observe a special phenomenon with my daughter. We were all in the family room, some reading books, others playing Battleship, and I was watching Ron Kenoly's video "God Is Able."

"Isn't that something?" I said to my daughter, fully expecting her to be caught up in the same spirit as I. She did not respond. "Dyane," I called out to her. No response. "Dyane!" I repeated a little louder. Still no response. "Dyane!!" I yelled. Although she was no more than eight feet from me, she still did not hear me. Her boyfriend, hearing my repeated outbursts, softly spoke to her, "Dyane, your Dad's calling you." She looked at me glazedly, and said, "Yes, Dad?"

I had just observed two things. First, the only voice my daughter could hear was her boyfriend's. Secondly, she had a smile in her eyes. I then realized that as a worship leader, I had just finished observing worship and had received two very important insights.

When I lead worship, whose voice am I listening to? Have I made sure that my ear has been tuned to the One I love so that when He speaks I can respond? Have I heard His voice? Do I know what He has said His heart is for that specific time of worship? It is easy to try to lead worship the way others would tell you to, trying to adjust to comments of "too long," "too short," "too fast," "too slow," "too loud," "too soft." In the midst of the complexities of worship leading, I am reminded to stay in the simplicity of worship. When I am in His presence, His is the only voice I hear. Therefore, before I lead others in worship, I must be sure that I have first of all spent time in His presence.

Finally, what is in my eyes when I lead worship? Again, it is easy to get caught up in all the technical and professional aspects of worship leading. The design of our sanctuary makes it as difficult to lead worship as it is to fly a Boeing 747, and sometimes it is easy to feel like ranting and raving as a ring master at a circus. Manuals have been written about the importance and necessities of "emoting" when leading worship. Emotion without existence is a facade. Existence without emotion is death. If I am to praise Him who is the help (and health) of my countenance, then my countenance should be displaying the joy of being in His presence. When I think about the Lord, when I look upon His beauty, do my eyes light up? When I lead worship, do I have a smile in my eyes?

David Baroni

Born in Natchez, Mississippi, David Baroni began playing piano at age five. He was raised with a variety of musical influences including Stevie Wonder, the Beatles, jazz fusion, Mahalia Jackson and Led Zepplin. David was led to the Lord in 1979 by Rita, who eventually became his wife. He traveled and did Christian concerts for about 10 years. During this time David composed such songs as "Soldier of the Light," "Keep the Flame Burning," "Carry the Torch," and "He is Here." Along with John Chisum, he co-wrote "O Mighty Cross," the title song of the Integrity Easter musical.

In 1992 David accepted the position of worship pastor at Bethel Chapel in Nashville. The church has recorded six live praise and worship projects called "Bethel Praise," which are now released on the Warner Alliance label.

David is a writer for Integrity Music and lives in Nashville with Rita and their three daughters.

So Much to Share

Before joining the staff at my present church, I traveled for about ten years doing concerts and praise and worship. One night at a New England Youth Retreat I was scheduled to sing a couple of songs in the evening service and then minister in concert in an "Afterglow."

This being the first time in front of these folks I was excited about the ministry opportunity and frankly hoping to move some "ministry units" — a more spiritual term for tapes and CD's.

The service progressed nicely. My first song seemed to be well received and the presence of the Lord was evident as we worshipped Him. Then it happened. The electricity went off in the middle of my second song! Fortunately I was singing at the piano, so when the lights and sound went out I kept on singing and leading the people in a worship chorus. As a few flashlights came on we continued worshipping. The whole atmosphere became almost like the catacombs and was conducive to heightening the spiritual sensitivity of youth and staffers alike.

Then someone shone a flashlight on the preacher and he delivered a powerful sermon with a mission emphasis. Several young people had an encounter with God they will never forget.

The electricity stayed off through the entire service so the "Afterglow" concert was canceled. I was thankful for the good service but a bit despondent about not getting to sing more. There would be no other opportunity at this retreat because I had to travel early the next day.

Though I confess I was more upset about the missed tape sales, I still presented my disappointment to the Lord in very spiritual terms. "Lord," I lamented, "how I wish I could have ministered to those young people. I had *so much* I wanted to share with them!"

Without chiding me for my misplaced motives or lack of candor the Lord immediately answered. I envisioned Jesus standing before me with outstretched arms as I heard in my heart His silent, sad reply, "How do you think I feel *all the time*?"

I pictured Jesus with His arms outstretched over Jerusalem, lamenting that the people had shunned a relationship with Him. I realized that if I, as a mere human, had felt like I had something to offer in a ministry situation, how much more does the Lord have to give to His people? Too often we go through life unaware of the presence of God when He is simply desiring for us to stop and have fellowship with Him.

Keep Thinking While Thinking Ahead

I've always tried to be prepared for a worship service. I prayerfully put the songlist together, always trying to be sensitive to the Holy spirit and let the music flow with what I perceive God to be speaking to the body. However, I'm also a firm believer in the "Victory of Vulnerability" — the power and approval that comes with spontaneous obedience. (Sometimes the best place for our plans are the trash can!)

One time in a service I was leading the hymn "Nothing But The Blood of Jesus." The congregation rose to their feet as their voices were lifted in praise. As we were singing I felt impressed to sing the Phil Johnson song, "Calvary, Calvary, Was It Meant For Him, Was It Meant For Me?" It was a special, poignant moment as we expressed our gratitude to the Lord for His love and sacrifice for us. Did I savor the moment? Oh no! While we were still singing "Calvary..." I was thinking ahead to still another relevant song, a song written by Carol Cymbala entitled "Mary's Song." This song tells the crucifixion story from a mother's perspective and it's very touching.

The only problem was that I forgot what song was already in progress. I came to just in time to hear myself singing "Calvary, Calvary is that my cross she's taking up Calvary?" I was horrified and mortified as the bewildered congregation sat back down. The moral of the story — don't forget what you're doing while you're thinking ahead!

Steve Kuban

Steve Kuban is an ordained minister with the Pentecostal Assemblies of Canada. He has been the director of worship and music at Crossroads Cathedral in Woodbridge, Ontario, since 1988. He is the president of Spirit and Truth Ministries, vice-president of Worship Resources International and an executive director of Canada Arise! (East) National Worship Conferences.

Steve is in high demand as a worship leader, teacher and speaker and has taught on praise and worship at national conferences in Canada, the U.S., Cuba and Guyana. His 15 years of worship leading experience make him equally at home leading worship in small church groups as he is leading at large interdenominational events such as March for Jesus, Canada Arise! and Billy Graham crusade rallies, some of which involve congregations of 10,000-15,000 or more.

Steve is an accomplished musical artist who began playing piano at age three, and worked as a professional secular musician from age 13. He studied music at Berklee

College of Music in Boston where, as an atheist, he was dramatically converted to Christ at age 18. As a Christian, he worked for many years in the professional music industry, but in 1983 God called him to full-time music ministry. He graduated from Northwest Bible College in Edmonton, Alberta, where he taught as a music professor for four years.

Steve and his wife, Judy, and their two children live in Toronto, Ontario.

Worship and Evangelism... in Cuba!

God's presence, more than anything else, is what testifies to the reality of the Gospel of Jesus Christ. We need never apologize for taking time in our services to allow God's Spirit to move, especially through our praise and worship.

I experienced this truth in a powerful way while in Cuba in 1993. My pastor, Doug Lynn, and I had been invited to speak at the first-ever, nationwide praise and worship conference in Cuba. The Cuban government had recently approved constitutional changes which allowed religious freedom for the first time in 33 years. The

Ministry of Religious Affairs had granted permission to the Cuban Assemblies of God to organize this historic conference. A total of 120 pastors, musicians, and worship leaders from all across the island had been hand-selected to attend this unique event. Many had travelled 800 miles or more in the backs of open trucks across dirt roads, enduring enormous hardships to be there.

As these worshippers came together, the atmosphere was electric with anticipation. It's hard for us in North America, with all our freedom to worship, to imagine the pent-up desire and intense longing of our Cuban brothers and sisters who had not been allowed to worship freely together in this manner for over 33 years. Within moments of the first worship song beginning, the intenseness of God's presence amid these worshippers was so overwhelming that we could only kneel and weep.

So much happened in the next four days that it would take an entire book to adequately describe it all. However, three events were particularly outstanding, for they convinced me beyond any doubt that God's presence brings people to Christ!

The concept of public evangelism was foreign to the Cuban Christians. Any religious activity outside of a registered gathering within a church building was prohibited. But God was about to demonstrate to them the power of evangelism through worship!

On the second day of the conference we shared the

principle that it is God's presence that draws men and women to Christ, and that it is through praise and worship that evangelism can take place. Immediately following this, everyone entered into a very high level of worship. As I was leading the people in worship, I noticed a girl walk through the back door of the church. By the way she was dressed it was obvious that she was a prostitute. She just stared around in utter amazement at what was happening. Then she pushed her way up through the crowded aisle of worshippers and stood right up at the front of the church, her gaze going from the overhead screen, to me, to the people around her, then back to the overhead screen. It was obvious that she was trying desperately to come to grips with what she was feeling and seeing.

One of the members of our team went up to her and told her about Jesus. This woman quickly accepted Christ and then began to weep uncontrollably. Within a short time, she was laughing and dancing with joy, knowing for the first time forgiveness of all her sin. It was an amazing transformation, and I remember thinking what a testimony of God's grace it was to see someone like this worshipping God with all her might on the front row of the church! It reminded me so much of the sinful woman who fell at Jesus' feet and poured out her love upon Him, having been forgiven so much (Luke 7:36).

But this was just the beginning! At about the same time, 25 high school students had been walking by the church, and, hearing the intense praise coming out through the open windows, were drawn into the service by the Spirit of God. They sat together in one long row across the balcony, watching intently as people continued to worship the Lord. After some time, the conference host took a moment and shared with them a brief gospel message and told them they could experience the same God we were joyously worshipping. An altar call was given, and 24 out of the 25 came forward to accept Jesus Christ as Lord! The delegates saw this and were amazed. Suddenly the thought that evangelism could not take place publicly in Cuba was replaced by the realization that evangelism *could* take place — through praise and worship!

And there was more! Later in the conference we were teaching about the power of worship and intercession, particularly the principle of praying God's blessing upon the nation and its governmental leaders. This was particularly difficult for many whose lives and families had been adversely affected by the past. But as they moved out in obedience and principles were applied in prayer, bondages of anger and hostility began to be broken and healing of past wounds miraculously took place. The level of worship and intercession reached a crescendo with an intensity that was indescribable!

As this awesome sound of worship and intercession poured out onto the streets, God caused another remarkable evangelistic occurrence to take place. At least 40 people walked into the church from off the street and stood tightly pressed together at the back of the church in total amazement. I remember so clearly the looks on their faces as they pressed in through the door, straining to catch a glimpse of what was happening inside this church. Later I discovered that many of those were nurses, doctors and professionals who worked at a hospital nearby. They had finished their shift and were on their way home. They had probably walked by this church time and time again, but that day something was different! God's presence was manifested in a dramatic way. The sound of worship and prayer was going forth, and they had been drawn in by what they had sensed.

Again, during the worship time a brief and clear gospel message was presented and people were given the opportunity to become Christians. Remarkably, all 40 of them came forward to accept Christ! This was no small matter. They knew that to become a Christian could seriously affect their job and family life. But for these people, God's presence was so real that they wanted Him regardless of any consequences!

That experience in Cuba taught me never to be concerned that public praise and worship might "turn off" the visitors in our churches. In fact, in my experience it has been exactly the opposite. I have seen over and over again that it is the presence of God that really draws people to the Lord, whether it be in our sanctuary, or on the streets of our cities, or anywhere else. God's presence, experienced through praise and worship, is so vital in these last days!

David Wayne Lawrence

Evangelist David Wayne Lawrence is a graduate of Oral Roberts University with degrees in music education and theology. He has a minor in psychology and has completed studies at Jersey City State College and Georgia State College in communications, audio engineering and business management. David has taught for over 25 years in institutions like Oral Roberts University, University of Arkansas, Jersey City State College, Kean College, Beulah Heights Bible College and many learning institutes overseas.

From his vast experience, David has developed seminars and home study courses through which people of all ages can learn many practical principles of music very quickly. After 15 years of marriage (and seven children), he understands that adults generally have neither the time nor the patience to establish viable music ability. Because of this, David has designed his teaching to meet the needs of both children and busy adults, equipping them to worship God through music.

Rev. Lawrence and his wife, Antonia, are worship evangelists. God has anointed them to lead His people into His presence. After 10 years of pastoring, they now teach churches and their worship departments practical aspects of cross-cultural worship and a lifestyle of worship.

David and Antonia live in Atlanta, Georgia.

Are We All On the Same Page?

One of the biggest lessons that I had to learn in dealing with my worship team was that we all had to have the same understanding of what praise and worship is. We all needed to be reading from the same page.

Early in my experience in leading worship many team members thought praise and worship varied in depth based on a person's ability to sing better or worse than others. Others felt it was the type of song sung. Some thought it depended on how fast or slow the song was. And still others thought that it had to be an Integrity's Hosanna! Music recorded song to really qualify as praise and worship.

This really had me confused. All of us were from different cultures, and, therefore, I determined we based our interpretation of praise and worship on what we grew up with. I realized that there had to be some biblical foundation that would bring us all together. This situation caused me to really seek God for answers. The Lord began to speak to my heart through His Word and books by authors like Judson Cornwall, LaMar Boschman, Bob Sorge and E. Bernard Jordan. He also allowed me to meet worship leaders like Kent Henry, David Johnson, Jennifer Randolph, Keith Childress, Ray Hughes and LaMar Boschman. These people showed me that even though there is diversity of expression there is one foundational understanding of praise and worship.

Some of the principles I learned were:

1. We gather in the sanctuary to converse corporately with God, Who then responds to our worship in different ways, through various vessels in the Body.

2. It is not a song service, but it is an expression of our hearts to Him.

3. Music/song is the best way to get a multitude of people saying the same things, at the same time, for the same reason.

After recognizing our lack of understanding of praise and worship, I began to gather material from many different praise and worship ministries. After studying this material and getting a solid foundation in my own heart, I put together a course of study for my entire worship department. We took several months to communicate the principles of praise and worship with each other. Then we began to move in the things that we had learned.

This process brought us together in every area of ministry. We became closer friends. We understood what we were supposed to be doing and where we were taking the congregation. We led the congregation in offering praise and worship to the Lord, instead of entertaining the congregation. Our examples as worshippers made a difference to the congregation, thereby giving them proper role models. This also opened up opportunities for all of the team members to minister prophetically and in other spiritual gifts like never before.

I guess the most obvious thing was that everyone's attitude changed! Because we all now had a similar understanding, we were all on the same page. There was no more competition, just sincerity toward God.

Gerrit Gustafson

Gerrit Gustafson is a Bible teacher, songwriter, and advocate of wholehearted worship. Gerrit conducts seminars and conferences throughout the nation and abroad through Kingdom of Priests Ministries.

Having served Integrity's Hosanna! Music as music coordinator, creative team consultant and songwriter, Gerrit has written over 40 songs which have been recorded by Integrity. These songs include "There's Glory All Around," "Unto You," "Have Mercy on Me," "Only By Grace," "Into Your Courts" and "I Hear Angels." He is also involved in developing resources for worship in small groups.

Apprehended by God's call during his college years, he served as pastor and teacher for 15 years in churches in Colorado, Florida, Mississippi and Alabama. Gerrit and his wife, Himmie, have five children and live in Mobile, Alabama.

The First Time

I remember the first time that music deeply affected me. It was in Ft. Payne, Alabama, in the late '50s. I was about ten. My older sister, Gwen, brought home a record of the song "Theme from a Summer Place" with the Percy Faith Orchestra. The first time I heard it was like meeting someone you really want to get to know. Then and there, I made my plans to listen to it all by myself, sometime when Gwen was gone.

The time came. We weren't into sharing back them, so I had to do some sneaking around to locate the hidden treasure. When I found it, I convinced myself that Gwen wouldn't mind me broadening my cultural boundaries. I reverently took the 45 (no that's not a handgun; it's a kind of record they used to have) out to our living room to play on our old Magnavox.

Remember how you had to put the attachment on the spindle to play those 45's... and how you could move the arm off the record and the song would repeat over and over? Well, when I had it all set, I turned it on, lay on the floor with my feet propped up on the wall and drank in every note.

I'm sure you remember how the combination of those slow eighth-note triplets, the sweet strings sounds, the horns, and that haunting melody line would just get under you and carry you off to some distant place? It had the same effect on me too. It was my first high... I was mesmerized. I didn't want it to stop... but when it did, it would just start over again. And again and again. The only thing I had to worry about was the return of the big sister.

That first time of tasting the power of music was the beginning of a long relationship. School bands, stage bands, dixieland jazz, popular jazz, and then studying composition at Florida State University. That first taste at age ten was the first step of a journey to make music my life.

And then there was the first time I encountered the power of worship. It was in Tallahassee, Florida in the late '60s. I was about 20. About a year before, I had become a Christian through the faithful persistence of my college roommate, Bob Sutton. We used to have Bible studies in dorms or apartments, so it wasn't unusual that we were going to hear a Bible teacher in the meeting room of a bank building.

There were about 200 people there that night. Everyone seemed so enthusiastic and so genuinely glad to see one another. Derek Prince was the guest speaker.

His English accent punctuated everything he said with such clarity and authority. Looking around at everybody's rapt attention, I was impressed that what we were doing was probably very similar to the activities of the early New Testament church.

But what was about to take place transcended our time and space orientation even more. When the message was over, someone stood up and said something like, "Let's just lift our voices in praise." Maybe we sang some songs—I don't remember—but I do remember something happening that absolutely penetrated the core of my being.

At some point in the singing, those 200 people began to sound like an ethereal symphony of voices warming up. I remember analyzing the sound: it was very polyphonic—many different melody lines going on simultaneously; it was arrhythmic—almost no rhythmic definition; and there was no chord progression—all of the singing held together around a major chord with added 6th's and 2nd's.

I remember how the sounds would swell to a great and jubilant tone, and then, almost as if there were an invisible conductor, the sounds would subside, leaving us in a state of expectancy as though God were about to whisper something to our hearts. At one such point, two female voices rose above the heavenly hum and created the most lovely little duet I think I have ever heard.

Talk about being carried away...! I didn't have a category for this music. Maybe I had missed something in my music history class! And when did all these people get together to rehearse for this? Do they have this music at the record store? The only word I could find to describe it was "heavenly." I decided, "This must be what worship sounds like in heaven."

I'm not ashamed to say that I'm hooked. Twenty-five years later, I'm still addicted. I have tasted the powers of the age to come (Hebrews 6:5). And that first time was not the last time. I have heard that heavenly sound again and again. That first encounter led me to a decision: More than anything, I wanted to be around that sound and that atmosphere for the rest of my life. I want my music and my whole life to adapt to that sound... I want it to be on earth as it is in heaven!

Somewhere I read a true story of a man who had devoted himself to the study of insects. He was what is known as an entomologist. Once when he was several weeks into the study of a certain insect in one of the western states, the shadow of a great bird caused him to look up and see an eagle. He was captivated as he watched this eagle navigate effortlessly on the wind. He estimated that it was a full eight minutes and several miles of flight before he saw that eagle flap his wings the first time. "This," he observed, "is an amazing animal!"

After that experience, the entomologist lost his interest in insects. From that point on, he devoted the rest of his life to the study of eagles!

Likewise, the first time music really spoke to me

through my sister's 45 on our family's Magnavox was the first step in a journey to make music my life. But the first time I encountered the heavenly sounds of worship was the introduction to something even more wondrous—living life as a worshipper in the presence of God. And for that discovery, I am eternally grateful!

David Morris

David Morris is a graduate of Christ for the Nations Institute in Dallas, Texas. For seven years he served as music minister at Church of The King in Dallas, where he and his wife, Laurie, were members for 11 years. David and Laurie are presently ministers of music at Spring Harvest Fellowship in Colorado Springs, Colorado.

David also ministers extensively teaching worship seminars with an emphasis on practical application for worship teams and establishing corporate appreciation for our priestly design as worshippers. A gifted songwriter and musician, he was the worship leader on the Integrity's Hosanna! Music recording, "His Word," as well as several annual church worship recording projects.

David and Laurie and their four children currently reside in Colorado Springs.

No Clones

I remember when my worship leader first began to mentor me in the principles of worship leading. This worship leader whom I highly respect had such a brilliant way with words. While leading worship, he would always have some amazing little revelation to share about ministering to the Lord. Of course, this was based on his many years of experience. I had very little experience at this time so his method of leading was paramount to me.

In desiring to emulate his methods and techniques, I began to lose my unique and individual anointing. I was becoming part-two of him. As I continued to strive toward the arrival at some great plane of worship leadership, I found that I was really very unlike my mentor. I needed to break free of what was hindering me from pursuing the fullness God had for me in my own personal style of leadership.

One thing I always wanted to be was a great orator. But my gifts were more musical and vocal than they were verbal and exhortative. Finally, one day my mentor came to me and spoke a clear truth that completely set me free. In terms of my worship leading he said, "David, if you don't have anything to say, don't say anything! Just sing the people into the presence of God." Since that time, I have felt more freedom to lead worship from the standpoint of *my* gifts instead of others'. I no longer need to apologize for my perspective of God's presence while leading, as I am a singer and a musician, not an orator.

Although mentoring is an invaluable, biblical principle, the greatest caution must be taken not to be "absorbed" by the one who mentors. Learn what gifts God has given *you* and capitalize on them. Be less concerned with the gifts someone else has and more concerned with what the Lord has entrusted to you.

Stephanie Boosahda

Since her conversion at age 12, Stephanie Boosahda has been diligent in serving her risen Lord. She has been known to many as a contemporary Christian recording artist and songwriter with nine albums to her credit. Her songs have been recorded by many artists, including Amy Grant, Carman, Miss America, as well as featured as theme songs for the 700 Club and the Feed the Children programs.

In the past 10 years she has enjoyed functioning as chief musician and worship leader in churches planted by her and her husband. She has also served as a keynote speaker at women's conferences and major worship seminars nationwide.

Stephanie and her husband, Wayne, reside in Oklahoma City, Oklahoma and use their gifts for the Body of Christ through Inner Court Ministries.

Serve the Lord with Gladness

In remembering the many times of ministry over the past 18 years on the road, a few instances stand out in my mind, one in particular. It was a time when I learned the importance of maintaining my sense of humor even in ministry, and to "serve the Lord with gladness" (Psalm 100:2).

I was in a church in Kentucky (a very stuffy and stiff church at that) and I prayed that the Lord would "thaw out" the "frozen chosen" people before it was my time to lead them in worship and ministry. I was very anxious and worried about the service. I was concerned about how they would receive me in ministry because this particular group of believers was the most unresponsive group to whom I had ever ministered. I thought to myself, "if 'the dead in Christ shall rise first,' then this congregation will be the first to go!" (smile).

Well, anyway, one of the ushers seated me on the front row in a spot they had reserved for me. While I was being seated the senior pastor was going through a long and detailed introduction of me to the congregation. As he asked the congregation to make me welcome, I stood up and proceeded to the top of the stairs leading to the podium when these "frozen chosen" broke out into uncontrollable laughter. Much to my surprise, I had a sign stuck to my back side that said "SEAT RESERVED"! (big smile).

Yes, the Lord certainly did answer my prayer to "loosen up" this congregation, and He used me to do it! (Thanks a lot!)

Lesson learned: In this day and hour when we are faced with so much stress and anxiety, even in the ministry, we must learn to take God seriously but not take ourselves so seriously. Many people in ministry today are stressed out, uptight and over-anxious. They too often leave anything but peace in the wake of their presence. As worshippers, we are called to be instruments of His peace, love and joy. In order for you and I as leaders to be truly effective, our lives must reflect a balance of work, worship, rest and play... a rhythm of life! All our *service* for Him should flow out of our *sonship* or relationship with Him. We can then maintain a joy and contentment in serving our King, whether the situation is favorable or unfavorable. We can "be instant in season and out" (2 Timothy 4:2). In the midst of all our ministry, let us not forget to lighten up, chill out, and enjoy His love. Take Jesus and His work seriously, but be willing to laugh at ourselves, to laugh at life (knowing that He laughs at our enemies), and to realize "a merry heart will do good like a medicine" (Proverbs 17:22). We have the privilege of serving the Lord with great gladness!!

Kevin
Jonas

Kevin Jonas is a gifted singer and accomplished song-writer. He is presently serving as worship director of Christ For the Nations Institute (CFNI) in Dallas, Texas. He is also the director of CFN Music, the recording, publishing and distribution division of CFNI. Kevin is the founder and president of the successful Christian Songwriter's Association (CSA), an organization dedicated to the education and net-working needs of the Christian songwriting community.

As an artist, worship leader and conference speaker, Kevin has travelled throughout the United States and abroad to churches of all sizes and denominations. He has had the honor of leading praise and worship for leaders such as Reinhard Bonnke, Jack Hayford, Pat Robertson, Richard Roberts and Loren Cunningham. He has also participated as a guest worship leader for Texas Right to Life and the North Texas Praise Gathering.

Kevin and his wife, Denise, and their three sons reside in Dallas, Texas.

A Very Long Drive Home

The final chord has been played, the service is over, and an awesome sense of God's presence lingers in the room. As I make my way to the doorway, I am greeted by an excited group of people emotionally describing my "anointed" performance in the just completed service. There is a great feeling of satisfaction in seeing the impact I have made on the lives of those in my congregation. The respect and appreciation is almost overwhelming. By the time I reach the car, I am sure that I am in the center of God's will. The Lord is obviously pleased with my ministry today.

My wife and children are already in the car. As soon as I get in the car, I feel a sudden change in the atmosphere. An icy, cold shoulder is coming from the direction of my wife. I try to ease the tension by talking about the service.

"Honey," I say, "did you enjoy the service? I felt like this was one of the most powerful services we have had in a long time."

The only response I get is an angry glare from the one who is usually the gentlest and kindest person I know. Suddenly, I feel a huge knot rising in my stomach. What could possibly be wrong with her after a service like we just had?

After a tense few moments of silence, she then begins to "share" with me a comprehensive list of insensitive things that I had done since the day began. I had left her with the responsibility to care for our entire family. She had fed us, cleaned us, and clothed us, without one word of thanks. While I was having the time of my life in an "anointed" service, she was struggling to get the children to their classes and the nursery. While I was "praying" and "fellowshipping with the saints," she was changing diapers. An elder's wife had even treated her rudely and caused her distress all morning. And lastly, she had hurried to get the children back into the car without my help while all I had thought about was my "fan club."

Anger begins to rise in my heart. Why is she so hard to please? Why does there always seem to be a problem? Why can't she seem to receive like all of the other people in the church receive? Within minutes, a fight erupts and everything the Lord did in the service is wiped away. Neither one of us feels good at all! Both of us are dealing with bitterness and resentment over the insensitivity of the other. It is a "no win" situation.

This is a generalized story of one of the most common problems I have dealt with as a minister and worship leader. Almost every person I know in ministry has battled the same problem. It is difficult to be the recipient of praise and admiration from those in your congregation and then feel the displeasure of the one you would most like to impress. It is equally difficult for the one that is not the "center of attention" to feel important or appreciated when you are the one that is always in the spotlight. This seems to be one of the primary strategies Satan uses against the family. Both people are working hard. Both are doing their best to take care of the responsibilities that they have. Yet both people feel like the other is insensitive to their needs. This makes for a *very long drive home!*

The answer to this situation lies in the ability of the couple to deal with each other according to "understanding." Pride is a primary obstacle to peace of mind and unity in this type of situation. Many arguments could be avoided if we would start looking beyond our own selfish pride and start becoming sensitive to the needs of our mate. Without a couple working together in harmony, there is ample room for the enemy to come in and sow seeds of discord.

The man is right in doing his best in the work of the ministry. He has, however, been unaware of his wife's struggles during the course of her day. While he was able to be with adults and feel appreciated, she was busy taking care of small children—many times a thankless responsibility.

The wife was right to take such good care of her family but she was also wrong, especially in regard to the timing of the sharing her frustrations. Proper and timely communication can be the missing ingredient to mutual appreciation.

True ministry should begin at home. Our ministry to others should be a reflection of what we experience daily in our homes. If we will begin to be aware of the needs of our mate, it will become easier to minister in peace. Our mates will then find it a joy to support us in the ministry God has given us to accomplish *to His glory.*

Brian Doerksen

Brian Doerksen is a first-generation Canadian, born in British Columbia and brought up in the Mennonite Brethren Church. As a teenager he began to experience a strong anointing as a songwriter and worship leader. After high school he attended a training school with Youth With A Mission, and later, he and his new wife, Joyce, settled in Langley, British Columbia, to work with the Langley Vineyard Christian Fellowship.

Over the years, Brian has led worship and taught at various conferences throughout North America, Europe and Asia in cooperation with organizations such as Vineyard Ministries International and Anglican Renewal. During this time he has been involved in many recordings of worship music. Brian's music calls the Church to seek a new level of intimacy with God and receive the transforming love of God. Some of his songs include "Refiner's Fire," "Faithful One," and "Father, I Want You to Hold Me."

Brian has been the worship pastor at the Langley Vineyard for six years and is presently the director of Pacific Worship School and executive producer of the musical drama, "Father's House." He and Joyce have three children.

Breaking the Fear of Man

Worship is all about people noticing God, not us. To be an effective worship leader, we must give up the desire to impress people and have them notice us. Because of this the Lord will sometimes ask us to do things to see if we fear Him more than the people before whom we are standing.

I vividly remember this happening to me. In fact I think it was the very first time I led worship for the conservative evangelical church I grew up in. They had asked me to lead worship for the Sunday night youth service. That night everything started out fine. Then the still small voice whispered to me, "Kneel down and worship Me." Inside I argued, "They *never* do that here... what will people think of me." It came again with more force, "Kneel down." I recognized that God was trying to break the fear of man in me. Finally I obeyed and there was a sweet release. I no longer led by singing and exhortation but by example, and this has been a key for me ever since. My desire is to build up the body through worship. I have found that I ultimately do the best job of this when I'm totally obedient to the Head of the Church, Jesus.

The Healing Presence of God in Instrumental Music

Music is a wonderful thing. It is something that God created to move all of who we are. Sometimes no words are needed. In fact sometimes they can even trivialize or cheapen the communication. This was illustrated to me powerfully in the last few years. In the summer of 1992 we hosted the "Worship Festival" here in Langley with Graham Kendrick, Bob Fitts, and other worship leaders from the Vineyard. During the very last session, I was leading worship and felt like the Lord had said to recommit our vows to Him. As we neared the end we began an instrumental piece I had written called "Rest in Me." After this song we planned to go into "Song for the Bride." As we began, I sensed I should call my wife onto the stage with me and that I should hold her while the music played as a picture of the intimacy Jesus, the groom, wants to have with his bride. Not a word was spoken, but the truth and emotion of God's love was powerfully communicated through the simple music and act. Many people cried and sensed the nearness of the presence of God.

Another time I was leading worship for the evening service at the Anaheim Vineyard while I was in town doing a recording. As many people came to the front for ministry at the close of the service, I had an impression that many of these people had wounds. God wanted us to play healing notes over them. I turned to my electric guitar player, Brian Thiessen, and briefly explained what I sensed. He then began to play notes. Long sustained notes. Sometimes he would repeat a note twice or he would play a different note. Amazingly I observed different notes had different effects on different people. Later I talked with several people who said whenever a certain note was played they felt a "healing presence" enter them.

Music is a powerful tool in the hands of God to bring life and healing. I believe more and more we will see what David saw when he played for King Saul. As worship leaders we should sometimes be careful not to fill the air with so many words so that the music can do its healing work.

Simplicity, Brokenness and an Out of Tune Piano

It was another hot day. The air was so thick our clothes stuck to our bodies. We were riding on the back of a tap-tap, the common public transportation in Haiti, where I had come for a short-term mission experience. After several hours we reached our destination, a town in the center of Haiti. Days like this make you ask questions like, "What am I doing here? Did God really call me to come on this trip?"

We had not been able to make previous arrangements as to where we would stay, but a missionary family graciously let us stay with them. By this time it had been quite a while since we had a time of worship together. We understood instruments were quite rare in Haiti, but they told us they had a piano in the chapel. We went right away so we could have a long-awaited time of worship and refreshment. I sat down at the piano and started to play. It was completely out of tune. I mean totally!

I immediately sensed the Lord speak. "Will you worship Me anyway, even with the out-of-tune piano?" I found one octave with relatively in-tune bass notes, began playing one note at a time and singing. Immediately the presence of God was evident and my tears began to flow. It was one of the sweetest times of worship I've ever had.

The truth is, I guess we are a lot like that out-of-tune piano. Yet God is still able to play his melody of love on our lives despite our weaknesses and failures.

In the middle of the push for excellence in worship music (which I wholeheartedly endorse) I'll never forget that sometimes the most powerful things come through broken people and whatever we've got. He's not waiting for us to get our "act" together so He can use us. He's waiting for our brokenness and humility.

LaMar
Boschman

LaMar Boschman is the author of four best-selling books on worship including A Passion for His Presence and A Heart for Worship. He also writes columns and articles for Ministries Today and Worship Leader magazines.

LaMar is the dean of the International Worship Leaders' Institute in Dallas, Texas, and concentrates on equipping church leaders from around the world. He has been a Bible teacher and international conference speaker for over 18 years, ministering with special emphasis on worship and the ministry of music.

LaMar has led worship on several worship recordings including releases from Integrity's Hosanna! Music and Cherub Records. He is the composer of numerous worship songs and the president of Worship Heart Music. Additionally, he serves on the advisory board of the North American Summit on the Future of Worship and as an advisor for the National Conference on Music and Worship.

Along with his wife, Teresa, and their two sons, LaMar resides in Dallas, Texas.

God Was There

Have you ever been leading worship and were so overwhelmed with the awareness of God's presence that you lost control of your emotions? It happened to me and I will never forget it. It was a very awkward moment—losing my composure in His presence—yet isn't that our goal?

I was leading worship at the International Worship Leaders' Institute in Dallas, Texas. We had gotten quite a ways into the songlist and everything was going great. We began to sing the passionate song, "Take Me In." We had sung it a few times and then I signaled to Tyrone Williams to began to play extemporaneously on the soprano sax and I sang softly into the microphone and worshipped the Lord spontaneously.

As I began to hear the sax express with feeling and emotion what was in my heart I broke and began to sob. I was overwhelmed with love for the Lord and burst into appreciation and thankfulness to Him. It so impacted me that I fell to my knees and bowed my head to the ground and cried. It was then that I sensed the presence of the Lord around me and on me. At that moment I was no longer a worship leader but a worshipper abandoned to God. There was no worship leader now; we were in the presence of God—face to face. The service was out of control of men. No human leadership was necessary or appropriate. Had anyone prophesied or pulled that meeting in another direction it would have been tasteless and grossly out of order.

I remember some of the thoughts that I had as a worship leader bent over on the platform, my face wet with tears and my nose dripping on the carpet. "What is everyone else doing?... Should I look?... No, I don't want to. God, You are so awesome. I want to stay here forever... Should I stand up and continue singing and leading the people?... Should I wait a little longer?" I finally decided to wait awhile and let the Lord finish what He had come to do. I have learned that it ruins the encounter and cuts it too short when the worship leader or pastor begins to speak direction to the meeting. Even an altar call at this moment becomes inappropriate. The Lord is already speaking profoundly to every heart. We pray for these kind of supernatural-power encounters, and then when they come we often kill the moment by touching it with our great, so-called inspired, ideas.

It is always my focus as a worship leader to lead the people to that kind of divine meeting with the Lord.

What does it profit anyone simply to sing songs for forty-five minutes. Worship leaders are to lead people—not in songs—but to Jesus. The purpose of worship is to invoke the presence of our exalted Lord.

Finally, after about fifteen minutes (which seemed like a long time as a worship leader but not long enough as a worshipper) I stood up and wiped my face. (Always have facial tissue close to the team and the congregation.) I led them in the song again. "Take me in to the holy of holies, take me in by the blood of the Lamb..." I noticed that the people in the congregation were on their faces too, without any direction from the platform. Slowly people began to stand up and sing with me. I didn't want to rush them. We just sang softly until they wanted to rise and sing as well. As worship leaders we should never force these moments into another direction or hurry the people. Transitions should always be slow in worship. When we talk after a moment like this our voices are soft and the spirit of our words should be that of our hearts, broken and contrite.

What does a worship leader do after this kind of encounter? Where do you go after this? What transition would be in order? My only options were to sing another soft worshipful song or respond in prayer. I began to pray and tried to sensitively verbalize what we were are experiencing and communicate to the Lord our response.

Worship's fruit is the presence of the Almighty in our lives. As worship leaders, we must be sensitive to allow

God to enter our services and do what He came to do. He can even lead His people without us telling them what to do. The key is to take the time to listen to Him and follow His direction.

Steve Ingram

Steve Ingram is an accomplished musician, producer and arranger. While his technique and touch on the acoustic piano have put him in demand as an accompanist, his expertise with the keyboard and digital technology place him in a rare group of Christian musicians. Steve has released a trilogy of meditation tapes based on the Scriptures entitled "Sounds of Love," "Sounds of Joy" and "Sounds of Peace."

Educated at Florida State University and Valdosta State University, Steve has taught a School of the Psalmist for the past 10 years, graduating hundreds of students from around the world. Prior to his own teaching and music ministry, Steve directed Kenneth Copeland's music department and arranged many musical projects including "He Is Jehovah" and "In His Presence."

Steve and his wife, Cheryl, currently reside in Daytona Beach, Florida. They are both licensed and ordained through Kenneth Copeland Ministries, and Steve serves as *the North Florida Area Director for the International Convention of Faith Ministries. He is a writer and publisher member of the American Society of Composers, Authors and Publishers.*

Lifestyle of Worship

For some twenty years now my wife, Cheryl, and I have been married and involved in the call of our life, music ministry. Through the years I've seen many changes, and yet a simple, very profound process has been waiting at every turn. I'd like to share it with you.

When we first met and discovered our love for each other and the Lord, we were both well entrenched in the "Jesus Movement." There were many kinds of musical groups, some now household names while others merged into mid-stream church life. Some of the more well-known included Chuck Girard and Love Song, Andrae Crouch and the Disciples, Danny Lee and the Children of Truth, The Archers, Honeytree, Petra, Second Chapter of Acts and our group, Alpenglow.

The typical ministry venue of the day was an open field with a flat bed trailer and a lot of extension cords hooked up to some farmer's barn—a Jesus Festival! There were always beach retreats, concerts and youth group lock-ins, but more than anything, we enjoyed an uninhibited, non-religious zeal for the presence of the Lord. Denominational barriers were not as visible nor even thought of as walls separating us. We were not just a few good performers with an audience watching but a vibrant, involved group of radical kids in love with God.

In late 1979, I moved my family to Texas to work as a music conductor and arranger for Kenneth Copeland, Bible teacher and evangelist. It was there that God began to solidify our future as a family and ministry. Jesus shared in Matthew 7:24-25: "Therefore whosoever heareth these sayings of mine, and doeth them, I will liken him unto a wise man, which built his house upon a rock. And the rain descended, and the floods came, and the winds blew, and beat upon that house; and it fell not: for it was founded upon a rock."

That's exactly what I wanted. I heard the Word and decided to obey. But oddly enough, with all my efforts, I found my life went the smoothest when I simply set my affection only on Him. I worshipped Him at home, in the living room, the kitchen and even while in the shower. Yes, there was a challenge to learn and experience the walk of faith (without which I will never please God, Hebrews 11:6). But the daily process of worship is my joy.

At this season of my life I began to really understand that my words do matter. I help create my future by agreeing with the Word or the spirit of this world, death. I even had to allow my mind to be transformed by it's renewal not by it's removal. Health, particularly in my wife's body, came as we both set ourselves in agreement with the Word and continued to daily worship God at home. Even when doctors said she could not have a child, our agreement brought great joy. Today, we have an alert, healthy, all-American, baseball-playing, piano-and-drum playing, blue-eyed, 13-year-old young man growing in our home, Steve, Jr. Our worship has become a lifestyle, not just an occasional religious coda to a day.

Recently, I have begun to realize again, as in my earlier walk with the Lord, that Jesus really does want to tabernacle with us. Great joy can reside in a home where Jesus is allowed to be present not only at bed time but all the time. Praise and worship of the Father through Jesus becomes a daily lifestyle not just a weekend experience. As I've reflected on the many wonderful spiritual and musical experiences of my past, I'm continually reminded of Jesus speaking of his Father in John's gospel: "But the hour cometh, and now is, when the true worshippers shall worship the Father in spirit and in truth: for the Father seeketh such to worship Him" (John 4:23).

Now we're in the midst of the '90s. Change is everywhere. The wall of Communism is down. Perverted politics and rights for every creature except an unborn child seems to be the norm of the day. Radicalism appears only confined to the weird. Even your church changes. People and members come and go. In fact, even you and I change. Still, stay alert and set your affections on the Lord. Don't despair and don't lose confidence. Become radical and unashamed of your love and devotion of the Lord. He's always there. He doesn't change.

Recently I saw a print advertisement that sort of summed up life these days. It was selling a particular music selection. It went like this: "This is the day that the Lord hath made but at the moment it totally stinks. There you are, a happy, content Christian, when suddenly your Visa bill comes in, your daughter doesn't make cheerleader and your in-laws decide to drop in for dinner. Fortunately there is a music for imperfect days and an imperfect world." The advertisement goes on to share an offer for some good Christian music.

I'd like to tell you that the process is always easy, but it's not. There are days of rain and days of sun. Fun days and not so fun days. I will assure you, though, our Father is not looking for worship but worshippers. He wants you and your heart, not some dedication to a memorized formula called the eleven-o'clock-worship-hour on Sunday. He's not mad at you. He's just waiting for you and I to come home like the prodigal in Luke 15.

Come home where there's constant love and joy. In Dad's house there is always great dancing and music. Make worship a part of your everyday life. Allow the process of being a worshipper to have its full effect.

Kim Clement

Kim Clement was born in South Africa and functions in the five-fold ministry office (Ephesians 4:11) as a prophet. He operates under the spiritual covering of Covenant Church of Carrollton and Pastor Mike Hayes.

Kim's ministry is marked by anointed praise and worship. The gifts of the Spirit flow with accuracy and bring liberty to God's people. Many are healed and set free.

Gifted with a musical background, Kim studied classical music through Trinity College of Music, London. He won the South African Award for best keyboard artist in 1972 and wrote the musical score for an Australian movie, "A Winter's Tale." Now God uses Kim's music in a special way: to prophesy from the strings.

Kim and his wife, Jane, and their three children live in Durban, South Africa, and reside in Dallas, Texas, when Kim is ministering in the United States.

Spiritual Songs, Saved Souls

A time of praise and worship creates a power-charged atmosphere that can change unbelievers. When our spirits break free in praise and worship, something happens in us that the world doesn't understand or recognize. But unbelievers know that what they're sensing is not soulish or intellectual—and something inside them cries out for it.

This was illustrated in a dramatic way when I was in Australia for a series of meetings. After holding a number of mini-crusades in several churches, we combined the congregations for a larger, two-night event at an entertainment center in Perth. More than 4,000 people attended each night.

That whole week I'd been teaching that when believers start singing "spiritual songs" (Ephesians 5:19), we go beyond the soulish realm into the spiritual realm. What we have in the Spirit is far greater than what the world has to offer, which can only appeal to the soul. Even though our souls may be moved by the music of such great entertainers as Barbara Streisand or Stevie Wonder, the "song of the Spirit" has a dimension and appeal that the songs of the world can never attain to.

My own church grew because we tapped into the dimension of singing spiritual songs. We would sing five or six choruses, and suddenly everybody would start singing in unity in the Spirit. This was not necessarily "in tongues," but rather words and melodies that came from believers' hearts in a spontaneous way. We found that during those times, unbelievers felt something they'd never experienced before—a spiritual atmosphere which drew them, ultimately, *into the kingdom.*

A well-known Australian punk rock group was in town at the time and heard about my message. I had addressed what I called "Satan's anointing" in worldly rock music—an anointing that often causes people to undress or become violent. I explained that those things happen because that's the nature of Satan. Conversely, when we start singing in the Spirit, we start challenging the kingdoms of darkness, and God clothes people with righteousness.

This teaching stirred the punk group to approach me with their own challenge. "We'd like to go on television with you before a live audience," they said. "We'll play our music for 30 minutes and see what manifests. Then you can come on for 30 minutes, and we'll see what happens when you do the kind of singing you speak about."

My first thought was, "Oh, me and my big mouth!" But instead I responded, "I'd love to!"

So, we went on television. Hundreds of people filled the audience, most of them friends of the punk rockers. The group played their music for 30 minutes and, of course, the audience began screaming and dancing. One woman started stripping. Then it was my turn. I played a little bit of music with a jazzy tempo and then began to worship God. The songs I sang were unrehearsed songs of the Spirit.

The Bible says that when Jehoshaphat's enemies were coming against him, his army sang—and then they sang. The first kind of singing was premeditated; the second was not. The Holy Spirit fell on the soldiers, and the result of their singing was that God was able to manifest ambushes against their enemies. Now God was telling me the same thing: "Hey, you don't have to fight this battle. All I'm asking you to do is lay down your sword, lift up your voice and praise Me!"

For about 10 minutes I closed my eyes and simply worshiped the Lord. When I opened my eyes again, I saw young people all over the floor weeping and crying. A genuine outpouring of the Spirit had occurred in front of the TV cameras! About 80 people were saved just as a result of that manifestation.

So often we think we must reach our culture by understanding the "language" of it. There is some validity to such a strategy. But the fact is, an unbeliever's language or culture does not have to be a stumbling block.

When you start manifesting the awesome, universal power of the Spirit of God through worship, people recognize it. And they respond.

Michael Green

Michael Green is co-pastor and minister of music at Faith Church in New Orleans. In 1987 he was the worship leader for the historic Congress on the Holy Spirit in the New Orleans Superdome. In 1990 Michael resumed this role in the Indiana Hoosier Dome with over 20,000 in attendance each night. He also frequently functions as worship leader, soloist and speaker for numerous conferences.

Michael has released five solo albums and has produced and been co-host of over 3,000 television programs. His extensive radio experience began at age 14 with a live, daily talk program.

Michael is a contributing editor for **Ministries** **Today,** *with articles on worship and the church published regularly. He and his wife, Linda, and their two sons live in New Orleans.*

Three Keys to Keeping Your Job

They say, "With age comes wisdom." Well, not always. Probably a better way to explain would be to say, "With experience comes wisdom."

By this time, I've been plugging away at this job for over 20 years, (I look fairly good for all of the wear and tear) and I can certainly say that I *see* things and *do* things quite differently than I did in the seventies and early eighties.

Call it mellowing? Maybe. A bit more realistic? Definitely.

Of course, I realize I've been at a disadvantage. I've had to stay in the same place. Restructuring, rebuilding, adapting to job transfers, adjusting materials to the skill levels of the folks God has given to us. Really, it's pretty unglamorous.

Oh, how I wanted to get my seminar honed, moving from place to place telling struggling folks how to do it. But, no. I've been in one place trying to make it work through frustrations and expectations. Yes, I've been close to burn-out at least once a year for twenty years. But, what do you do? You just keep plugging away.

Sure, it hasn't all been easy, but there have been gratifying moments, and through it all the most important lessons have been the "people" lessons.

Over the years, I've noticed some ministries that seem to specialize in being impersonal or even clinical in their relationships to people. Perhaps in the short term you can get a few good miles out of that mode of operation. But, as years pass, you realize there must be relationship.

At times, we have all been like the cartoon of Charlie Brown where he says, "I love mankind, it's people that I can't stand!" Yes, we love the concept of ministering to the Body, it's just dealing with this particular group of less-than-cooperative sheep that is the problem.

Periodically, God does give you a fresh touch and a vision for your ministry and for the people that He will entrust to you. Those times of recharge are special times, indeed.

Here are three key points to help you get encouraged and recharged. These points will help you survive the rough times.

• **Work on your people skills.**

Happy, dedicated off-key people are much easier to deal with than an "on-key lynch mob." Take time to share the dream. Give them small pieces and commend them with each learning step. Don't talk down to them; lift them up! I heard it said once, "People have a way of becoming what we encourage them to be, not what we nag them to be."

Realize that they have pressures, needs and struggles. You have been thinking about that music for a few days and your creative juices are flowing. You also know where you are going with the direction of the music. On the other hand some of your folks are doing good just to get there. They've gobbled fast food, fought traffic and are a bit frazzled. Work them in easy.

It is especially important to develop strong relationships with those of stronger personalities. Every group will have one or two folks whose leadership and persuasive skills are stronger than the rest of the group.

Some leaders fear these folks and they, out of sometimes not knowing exactly what to do, fail to build a good relationship and thus the strong person becomes a liability to the program. Build a fence of kindness around these folks. Use *their* strengths. Remember the old self-defensive advice: "Use your opponent's weight against them." Get these people on-board and many other good folks will be swept along in their currents.

Also, know you can't treat everybody the same. The guy who espouses that philosophy usually moves every 18 months looking for the perfect place or he just has his wife and kids singing with him (...with teeth clenched, no doubt!).

Everybody and every group is different. Some need

prodding, some need an ear, a pat on the back, a smile, a "What happened at your son's game? I hear he's quite a pitcher!" or "I really need your help, can I count on you?" Get the idea? Take care of these folks. They will take care of you and they will even get better!

• **Adapt your material to the skill level of your people.**

This one area can get quite sticky. It is also an area where you must subjugate your own taste for the overall betterment of the team. You might love the "Brooklyn Tab" sound, but if you've only got one baritone, trying to be tenor, you can forget it. Understand?

One of the greatest natural examples of this concept of knowing your players and their skills was former Redskin coach, Joe Gibbs. Three Super Bowl rings verify that the guy knows his football, but even more striking to me is the fact that he did it with three different quarterbacks with three distinct styles. A good coach evaluates his talent well; then he proceeds.

Since 1975, I've presided over five manifestations of the choir and praise singers... some better than others. We seem to go through distinct phases every few years.

It is just as important to know what your people *can't do* as well as what they *can do*. This part becomes easier as the program grows but with small groups in smaller churches it is vital.

What is your strength? Soloists, small ensemble, trio, duet, instrumental? Start there and add as you go.

- **Lighten Up!**

Yes, we are serious about our call and the business at hand, but there is no need to stomp around with that "I'm the only one carrying the load around here" look.

After the tedious rehearsal time, after the labor and agitation, before the big performance I usually say something profound like, "I thank you for all your work and dedication. You're good folks. Now, just forget the notes, the words and all the technical stuff. Let's just go minister and let's have fun doing it. Let's go!"

As long as God gives us the folks to care for, expect the unexpected. It won't be dull, and if you stick to it, you will be surprised at what God will do. Those old toads just might turn into kings and priests!

Finally, the worship service is a joyful culmination of many variables and our responsibilities are both sacred and secular. Sometimes, it is not an easy job to balance them all, but with God's help and a willing attitude on our part, we can make it.

Be encouraged. Do great things for the Kingdom.

Daniel Amstutz

Daniel Amstutz is currently serving as the pastor of worship arts at Power Community Church in Anaheim, California, pastored by Tom Barkey. Daniel moved to California in August of 1990 with his wife, Tracy, and their two children.

Daniel is a pastor/teacher, songwriter, and author, and also ministers prophetically. Before relocating to California, Daniel served for seven years under pastor Bob Yandian as the minister of music at Grace Fellowship in Tulsa, Oklahoma. While at Grace, Daniel organized an annual teaching seminar called The Local Church Music Seminar, and recorded five worship tapes called "Singing With Grace," which the Lord has used to bless many people.

As the president of Face to Face Ministries, Daniel ministered nationally and internationally for about 12 years. He is currently making preparations to serve as a senior pastor where the Lord leads.

Merry-heart Medicine

I grew up in church. I have been involved in church as long as I can remember. My mom and dad pastored for many years in several Baptist churches. Consequently, I have been around ministry literally all of my life. During this time I have seen and experienced so many things that I have often been jokingly encouraged by friends to write a book. Let me share a few of my experiences with you.

I should preface my thoughts by saying that although some of the situations seem extremely comical now, at the time they happened some of them did not seem the least bit funny.

For seven years I was on the staff at a large church in Tulsa as minister of music and worship leader. During one service there was a strong anointing and we had had a wonderful time of worship. During the worship a lady began to prophesy. She started out okay. Her words were something along the lines of, "Oh my children, I love you so much and desire to give you My best." However, as she continued, her "prophetic" word went downhill quickly. "Oh, yes I desire to give you good gifts and come to you just like the Easter Bunny! Why, yes! I am even like Santa Claus and will bring you good things. And I know if you've been naughty or nice..."

I was so shocked and horrified at what I was hearing. I had my own drama playing in my head entitled, "Help! What Do I Do Now?" I could feel my ears turning red, from the top down! I managed to take charge and stopped her mid-sentence. I gently corrected the situation, and tried to encourage the people to worship the Father again. I exhorted them that He was the true giver of every good and perfect gift. However, even as I did this I saw several people softly elbowing their neighbors and pressing their lips together, trying not to laugh.

During one service where I was leading worship I had been kneeling and had been quite caught up with the presence of God and His awesomeness. Suddenly I felt a touch on my right shoulder. Honestly, my first thought was that God had sent an angel to tell me something. I struggled to open my eyes a bit, and, to my utter surprise, I found a lady standing next to me with a huge Bible under her arm. We had an excellent ushering staff at this church, and I was shocked that she had gotten past all of them and had even managed to walk up all eight steps leading to the platform.

I looked at her and said, "Yes?" as if I were in slow motion. She told me that she had "a word for the people," as she lifted up her huge Bible. I could only get out the word, "Yes?" again in slow motion. As it turned out, she felt that she had been given the ability to heal people by simply "speaking the word." So she did just that. She spoke one word into the microphone, "Kidney!!" (She thought it was a word of knowledge for a healing).

I remember thinking, "This is a nightmare! This is not happening to me! God *help!* What do I do?" She later showed up at another smaller committee-type meeting and right in the middle of the speaker's talk, blurted out the word "kidney," followed by "spleen" and several other organs. She was corrected, and eventually delivered of a demonic spirit. However, the lady will be long remembered, I'm sure, and I have learned to keep one eye slightly open!

Then there was the time one of my worship leaders' panty hose rolled down her legs, all the way to her feet, as she walked up the platform of Bible School Chapel to sing special music. And the time one young lady on my worship team was dancing in praise to the Lord as her slip literally fell off onto the floor! She never missed a beat. She simply bent over and scooped it up and danced off the platform. Or how about the time one of our most faithful trombone players got sick in the service and threw up in the bell of his trombone, right during worship. Most of the people never knew, but the brass section sure did! Then there was the night when someone in the congregation had just sneezed very loudly during a quiet time, when I was verbalizing my praise to the Lord by saying, "Bless You!"

Another time I was leading worship and noticed my pastor giving me strange hand signals with a frown on his face. At first, I thought he didn't like the song we were singing, but when he came up on the platform, stood next to me and interrupted the worship, I knew something was wrong. Only later did I learn that the violinist directly behind me had somehow caught her violin bow on one of the buttons of her blouse, and one by one, they proceeded to pop open, with every stroke of her bow.

What have I learned through it all? A few things: like to keep going and not take yourself too seriously. Learn to laugh during the rough spots, and don't beat yourself up when things don't go quite right. Many times we have rehearsed and worked so hard to have everything just right, only to have seemingly everything go wrong.

I've also learned that we serve a mighty God who is bigger than whatever may go wrong. So be encouraged, fellow worshipper. If you start to grow weary in well doing, maybe it's time to take a little "merry-heart" medicine and laugh!

Len Mink

In 1969 Len Mink had his own musical variety television show in Cincinnati, Ohio. Later he went on to co-host a top-rated local (Cincinnati) daytime talk show. During this time Len appeared on several well-known network programs . He was also featured in 43 pops concerts with the Cincinnati Symphony Orchestra.

Despite his successful career in the entertainment field, there was an area deep within him that show business was unable to fulfill. In October of 1971, Len began a personal relationship with Jesus Christ that filled that void. Shortly after that Len was diagnosed with a terminal blood disease and given only a few years to live. God miraculously healed him, and he was given a clean bill of health by his doctors.

Since that time Len and his wife, Cathy, have been involved in a full-time evangelistic ministry, sharing the power of Jesus Christ through the Word and song. Len has an outreach to children through his "Gospel Duck" children's *series. He also works with Kenneth Copeland, leading worship in his crusades.*

Len and Cathy and their two children live in Cincinnati.

Don't Fence Me In

More times than I can remember I have been worshipping God in an unusual or different surrounding and found myself in the awesome presence of God. It happened under a palm tree with no musical accompaniment except wooden drums, clapping hands and beautiful multi-level harmonies. I had a similar experience on an ice flow, huddled around an oil heater, as we raised our hands to the Lord in worship. It has happened to me in prison, on a motorcycle, diving the Great Barrier Reef, in a group of four-year-olds, and, yes, occasionally in a church.

I am convinced this awesome presence of God is what every rock singer and entertainer is really looking for. We were created to worship God. It is woven into our fabric whether we respond or not. Music was given to worship God. Money, talent, resources of any kind and every kind were given by God with the intent of worshipping Him. We are fashioned with space inside that can be satisfied only with a rich, full-time relationship with God through Jesus Christ. No other thing or person can fill that space.

We are such creatures of habit and predictability that we occasionally suffer from what I call the inoculation effect. This happens when we become immune to the myriad levels of diversity with which God wants to flow through us to express worship back to Himself. We tend to "formula-ize" the worship experience, settling for much the same warmed-over material and methods service after service. By doing this we seldom challenge ourselves, much less anyone to whom we are ministering. We are too often ruled by rejection, tradition, fear and an I-don't-want-to-offend-the-main-supporters-of-the-church attitude. This causes a religious spirit to set in and the rest, unfortunately, is very predictable: no power, no joy, no spiritual nourishment, no changed lives and no fun!

I find myself more and more with a craving for God to show as many facets of His character and personality as possible through my life. We are talking about a covenant relationship with the Source of infinite creativity, endless expression and fathomless ability. The miracle of it all is that God can take my little one-milliwatt worship signal and, as I up-link to Him, amplify, magnify and direct that signal into something tremendous (sounds like loaves and fishes to me!).

After a few years of wandering, I came to my present home of Cincinnati, Ohio, to start a job. I had been raised in the coal fields of southwest Virginia and was accustomed to hearing folk and bluegrass music ringing through the hills. I remember how it stirred my heart. I knew even then that music was one of the most powerful forces on earth, and I was drawn to it like a moth to light. However, even with this background I had only heard symphonic music occasionally on the radio late at night. I will never forget the first time I attended a Cincinnati Symphony concert. When the symphony exploded into the first piece they were playing, I burst into tears and sobbed like a baby. Something deep inside me was trying to articulate, "All this is somehow supposed to connect with God."

Our worship of God must seek to be as exciting, varied, real and creative as God Himself. We should use all the tools we have available to honor the Lord. And we must seek to tap into the Source of all creativity, God Himself, to fully give expression to our worship.

We must throw away our confining ideas about worship and seek to glorify our King in new and creative ways. I'm not sure, but God may have inspired that famous Broadway song from "Oklahoma," "Don't Fence Me In."

Tom Kraeuter

As managing editor of Psalmist Magazine *for over six years, Tom Kraeuter had the opportunity to hear the heartfelt needs and desires of those involved in the ministry of praise and worship. Combining this with his own experience in leading worship since 1977, Tom now teaches full-time at worship seminars, conferences and retreats across the nation as a part of Training Resources.*

Tom's first two books, Keys to Becoming an Effective Worship Leader *and* Developing an Effective Worship Ministry, *have been acclaimed by leaders in the praise and worship movement nationwide as vital, practical handbooks. Additionally, Tom's writings have appeared in such magazines as* Ministries Today *and* Worship Leader.

He is presently the minister of worship at Christian Outreach Church in Hillsboro, Missouri. He has served in this capacity since 1984, fulfilling the call of God on his life to "equip the saints for the work of the ministry" (Ephesians 4:12).

Tom, his wife, Barbara, and their three children reside in Hillsboro, Missouri.

Dwelling in Unity

Some time ago I was teaching a worship seminar at a church. To stress a particular point, I shared a story about a husband who had left his wife. At the conclusion of the story I noticed the worship leader from the church was noticeably crying. I considered stopping to pray for her, but I did not believe that was the right thing to do at the time. Later, during a break, I asked her about the tears. She explained that a while back her husband had left her. Not only had he left her but he had left her for a woman who was her cousin and who was also the youth leader at the church. He and the worship leader had married early in life and he had become everything to her. When he left she was devastated. She was so badly wounded that there were times she did not show up for worship rehearsals. There were even times she was absent on Sunday mornings—even when she was scheduled to lead worship.

This same church has an administrator for their worship ministry. This frees the worship leader to do what she does best and not be bothered with the details of organization. When the above scenario was going on the administrator approached the other members of the worship ministry with a choice: "We can either ask her to leave the team and totally devastate her life or we can help her through. Which one do you want to do?" Please understand that most of these people were not just passing acquaintances. They were close friends. And they chose to help her through.

So when she did not show up for rehearsals they went on without her. On Sunday mornings when she was supposed to lead and failed to appear, the administrator posed the challenge to the music team: "Okay folks, who's going to lead this morning?" In the midst of all this, they covered so well for her that, although the congregation was aware of her situation, they were completely oblivious to the depth of her struggle.

When the worship leader began to put her life back together she went to the music team and thanked them. "You'll never know what you did for me," she said. "You loved me when I was so unlovable. You helped me through the toughest time of my entire life. Thank you!"

At our church we have a Christian school, grades K - 12. Although my oldest son is only in third grade, our family frequently attends the school's varsity basketball games. Being a very black-and-white person I regularly disagree with the referee's calls. Usually my opposition is voiced only to myself or those around me, but occasionally, if I perceive the call to be really bad, I may be more vocal.

Interestingly, a friend of mine from our church is a basketball referee. He does not usually officiate at our school's games, but when he does I have found that I seldom disagree with his calls. As I began to ponder why this was so, I realized it was not necessarily that he did a much better job as a referee. The reason is that he and I have a relationship. It is more difficult for me to find fault because I know him and I like him. We are friends.

Awhile back, after ministering at a church, I went to lunch with the pastor. During the course of the conversation he mentioned that they had previously had a bit of friction between two members of their church's music ministry. The reason stemmed from the fact that one was very outspoken and often shared his feelings freely. The other person was much more reserved and did not necessarily want to hear the feelings of the other, especially as those feelings related to her ministry abilities.

After explaining the situation the pastor told me that the problem had been solved. "Do you know how we did it?" he asked.

"No, but I'd like to," I responded.

He explained that one day the entire music ministry team spent the day together at an amusement park. The two who were occasionally at odds with one another spent a great deal of time together during that day. They got to know each other. They became friends. The problem was solved because of their deepened relationship.

Strong relationships are essential to long-term ministry. If relationships are superficial, conflict will seldom be totally resolved. Relationships that are only at the surface level have no real commitment or loyalty. Without strong, healthy relationships, the music ministry of the church will almost always be in turmoil.

However, the converse of these statements is also true. When strong relationships with true loyalty and commitment are present, no amount of conflict or difficulty will rend them.

Psalm 133 says that God bestows His blessing when brothers dwell together in unity. No one ever told me that endeavoring to have solid relationships within the music ministry of the church could be so powerful. But it is. I have seen it repeatedly. And it will work in your church, too.

Tim Smith

For the past 25 years Tim Smith has dedicated his life to training musicians and worshippers around the world. He served for 12 years as music department chairman at Portland Bible College in Portland, Oregon, and directed numerous worldwide ministry tours with His Tapestry singing groups.

Tim has composed many worship choruses such as "Our God Is Lifted Up," "Mighty God," and "You Reign With Power." He has also authored the book, Piano In Worship. Tim's expertise ranges from leading worship seminars, writing, arranging, and conducting to private lessons on a variety of instruments.

Currently Tim has established SongSmith Ministries to further equip musicians and release worshippers in broader dimensions of praise and worship. Tim, his wife, Maryl, and their four children live in Aloha, Oregon, and minister at Living Hope Fellowship.

Worship Around the World

My position as a teacher at Portland Bible College gave me the unique opportunity for eight years to take small worship teams around the world. What a joy to experience the variety of "cultural" worship ranging from the fiery services in Brazil to the sweet but jubilant meetings in Indonesia and Malaysia (where their faith could put them in prison). And who could forget the quiet but powerful worship of the Japanese church (not to mention the raw squid or octopus!). We faced coal miners sweeping through the streets of Bucharest and then went on to be humbled as we observed the quiet strength of faith in the saints of Romania when they exercised their newly found freedom of public worship by the thousands.

In Ireland, in the middle of a worship service, we watched God melt the bitter heart of a man who had lost both legs to an IRA bomb. During worship in Wales, we saw two teenage witches leave while later thirteen of their younger friends got saved. We rejoiced as God supernaturally drew eight churches together for a night of worship in Hereford, England, and birthed an unprecedented sense of unity in that area. What a joy to see Maoris of New Zealand worshiping the one true God. In Australia we had to keep on our toes to stay up with the fresh, humorous and open style of the "Aussies."

Who would have thought in a conservative country like Finland, that God would be raising up such a beautiful group of radical worshippers. In Estonia, where hatred runs deeply between the Estonians and the Russians, we watched as God brought them together under His banner of praise. What a thrill to sing and dance together with hundreds of Russians in the Estonian border town of Narva, as we celebrated a common Lord.

When I consider these great and precious moments the Lord has given me, I am overwhelmed by the sense that something is being birthed in the world that is much bigger than a method or a movement or an organization. It is His people delighting in Him. It really is the earth being "full of the knowledge of the Lord as the waters cover the sea" (Isaiah 11:9). It is in this context that our leading of worship takes on a proper perspective. Rather than our own agenda, we are participating in a universal, eternal, divine gathering of His saints and yet relishing every delightful moment God brings to us no matter where it is or whether alone or with many.

One of my most treasured and vivid memories took

place in Rio do Janeiro, Brazil in 1987. Right before the evening service, I received a telephone call from a missionary friend telling me that my youngest daughter's appendix had ruptured three days prior and they had just found out and taken her into surgery. I called my wife immediately at the hospital in Portland. While I was talking to her they brought our daughter (Amy) out of surgery right by the phone. I got to pray for her over the phone from thousands of miles away. She had made it through the surgery fine, but we weren't sure yet of the prognosis.

I had to make a decision. Would I go in to the church and minister or stay and wait for more news? I felt God assure me that Amy was going to be okay and to go ahead with the evening as planned. What a great service! The Brazilians pull out all the stops and put our most radical services to shame. At the end of the service I felt compelled to challenge them to worship God with total abandonment. I challenged them to shout, clap, lift their hands, dance and generally be very physical in their expression of worship to God (something Brazilians love to do anyway) for five minutes without stopping and see what God might do in that atmosphere of praise. We sang a fast song in Portuguese and then broke into the loudest, most exhilarating time of praise you could imagine. Instrumentalists played out their hearts before the Lord; singers with whole-hearted adoration lifted up a great cry of praise to God; young ladies with tambourines gracefully stepped and turned among the hundreds of worshippers. The whole church seemed to be alive with choreographed ebullience.

I distinctly remember watching a tall young Brazilian with only one arm on the front row during the service. His face had glowed the whole evening as he seemed to be drinking in all the joy of God around him. And now, in the midst of great rejoicing, he was twirling and grinning, and yet there was one expression he obviously could not participate in. Before I really knew what I was doing, I had leaped to his side and lifted my right arm to match his. We proceeded with some of the most intensely spiritual "high-fives" you could imagine. Over and over until it hurt. I don't know how long that moment lasted, but the picture is burned into my memory as we shared tears and laughter, aching legs and red palms.

I suppose many applications could be drawn from this simple story. But I do know this: As I joined my brother—hand to hand—for that one moment, seemingly for the first time in my life I felt I was truly worshiping God.

And my daughter? The doctors called her the "Miracle Child."

John Chisum

Singer, songwriter and currently manager of song development for Integrity Music, John Chisum has been a music industry professional since 1984. Having served as a professional manager, vice-president of publishing, and vice-president of worship resources for Star Song Communications in Nashville, Tennessee, John joined Integrity Music in early 1992.

Perhaps best know for his songs recorded by Larnelle Harris ("Mighty Fortress"), Steve Green ("Call to Worship"), Gaither Vocal Band ("In the Heartland"), First Call ("Back to His Heart") and The Cathedral Quartet ("Can He, Could He, Would He"), John has also recorded his own solo album, three praise and worship albums with Bethel Chapel Records, and was the featured worship leader for Integrity's Hosanna! Music recording "Firm Foundation."

John and his wife, Donna, have a daughter and live in Mobile, Alabama.

There Really Is At Least One!

Having led worship over the years in many churches and with Hagin Ministries of Tulsa, I would never have thought the Lord would thrust me permanently and full-time into a decidedly worship-oriented career and ministry.

Donna and I had been married for just a little over three years and had endured just about as much local church music ministry as we could stand at the time. The first pastor I worked with as an Associate Pastor and Music Minister told me one day he had been praying and the Lord told him it was time I left. "Gee," I thought, "why didn't He tell me first?" The second pastor allowed the youth of the church to run all over everyone. The third wasn't, by his own admission, even called to pastor. And the fourth, well we never really got to the fourth. He offered us a job in Nashville and then withdrew the offer after we'd made all the arrangements to join him there.

After these first three years of marriage and extremely difficult circumstances Donna said to me one night,

"Honey, why don't we just go to Nashville and get *normal* jobs and be *normal* people?" By that time I wasn't really sure what normal people were, but I was willing to go try to learn! I often tell people that my favorite verse of Scripture during those years regarding pastors was, "There is none good, no, not one" (Romans 3:10, paraphrased).

We moved to Nashville in the late Autumn of 1983 and hit the streets looking for normal jobs. Donna found a graphics position and I found a paper route at three a.m.—no one wanted a burned-out music minister. It was less than three months later that I had my first song recorded and had signed an exclusive publishing agreement with Gary McSpadden and Bill Gaither, spinning my life into what is currently my tenth year in Christian music professionally.

Later in 1984 we were introduced to a young church south of Nashville called Bethel Chapel. Although skeptical of anything that resembled the type of churches we had cycled through the previous few years, we grew to love this fellowship, the pastor Ray McCollum, and the people who came to enjoy God's presence throughout each week. I would fill in as a worship leader from time to time, but I had no real desire to work even on a part-time basis with the worship ministry.

It wasn't until late 1988 that God's unique plan to restore us in ministry began to unfold. We had walked through a lot of restoration through the wonderful teaching of our pastor and we had faithfully attended, tithed, and served in other capacities in the church. The Lord had begun to lovingly confront me on deeper issues of my heart: resentments that stemmed from childhood abuse and other things that I was blinded to for various reasons.

During this period I traveled to England on business and experienced firsthand the ministry of a true prophet of God—rare these days, unfortunately. I was introduced to this man by a mutual friend, but, having never heard his name I had no inkling that he was indeed the most prominent minister in attendance that evening at this particular event. Just after we were introduced he told me the Lord had been speaking to him about me and he asked if we could have a word of prayer together. I thought "Oh, no! This guy is a real weirdo!" However, within thirty seconds of his prayer for me I began to experience the most powerful visitation from the Lord I have ever known and the impact of those moments works within me to this day.

The sum of what he spoke to me that night was a prophetic word of deliverance from not only the childhood issues of abuse, but the adult issues of woundedness and bitterness. From this trip I returned humbled and broken, ready to worship and serve the Lord in a new way.

Some months later in 1989 the full-time worship leader at Bethel Chapel stepped down for a ministry break of his own and I was asked to fill in for him until they could search out a new full-time worship leader. I still had no intentions to take this position permanently, but the first Sunday I led as interim, God blew the roof off, so to speak, as the congregation entered into worship on a level that had not been known by them at that time. I can take *no* credit for this! I don't remember praying very much or feeling the least bit spiritual as I went into that service. It was a sovereign act of God as far as I'm concerned, but the spark of that service grew into a flame that resulted in the writing of many worship songs over the next few years and the recording of five commercially released worship albums to date! I indeed became the full-time at Bethel Chapel from 1989-1992 and worked shoulder to shoulder with a brilliant worship songwriter, George Searcy (who wrote "Making War In The Heavenlies" and many others). The collaboration that we enjoy currently in songwriting grew out of our years together at Bethel Chapel, years that continue to bear good fruit as David Baroni carries the torch of local church worship into the mid-90's.

I don't believe I would be at Integrity Music as a writer, worship leader, and Manager of Song Development had it not been for the marvelous work of personal restoration that God brought to us through the local church and the ministry of a great pastor. So I now know, "There is one good—there is!" (Romans 3:10 reparaphrased by a restored man).

Don
Dalton

Don Dalton has been involved in leading and teaching praise and worship throughout the United States and 25 other countries for over 25 years.

Beginning at age 3, Don began singing in his father's revival meetings and their local church TV program. As a teenager in the late '60s, God began to birth in the youth group of his church a new type of worship music: songs with lyrics taken from Scripture. Out of that singing ministry was formed the group "New Creation Singers." God used Don and his wife, Valerie, to play a part in ushering in the current praise and worship movement. In all, they have recorded nine worship tapes, three on Sparrow Records. Many of the songs they recorded in the '70s are still being sung worldwide and have been used by Integrity's Hosanna! Music and Maranatha! Music.

Don has ministered at numerous worship seminars and conferences nationwide. His articles on worship have been published in Psalmist *magazine and in magazines from other nations.*

Don is now the pastor of Life Christian Center in New Braunfels, Texas, where he and Valerie and their two sons reside.

Owning the Vision

My earliest recollections of music come from the inside of my mother's accordion case! The red velvet lining seemed to be the most luxurious material I had ever encountered, and the unique smell that only an accordion could produce was special indeed. I remember playing inside (occasionally closing the lid to create the ultimate hiding place) while my Dad played the guitar and Mom the accordion as they rehearsed songs like "The Old Rugged Cross" and "What a Friend We Have in Jesus."

My father, who was an evangelist, began involving my sister and me in his ministry when we were both young. I remember singing in his revival meetings and our church's local TV program when I was about four. My repertoire consisted of songs like "Let the Sun Shine In," "Love Those Kiddies With the Curls on Top," (I had curls) or "You're Not Too Small." Although I have no idea who wrote them, they had very strong lyrics that presented a clear gospel message.

I remember falling asleep on many a church pew or in the back seat of our Nash Rambler while driving home from a revival meeting a hundred miles from home. I also remember when I was four years old sitting in a service listening to my Dad preach about hell and suddenly realizing I would go there unless Jesus was in my heart. I gave my heart to Him that night!

I continued to be involved in my Dad's ministry until I was 25 years old and have continued in ministry to this day. As I look back at those years now, I believe one of the important things my parents did was to make me feel a part of the ministry. It wasn't just Gene Dalton's ministry; it was the Dalton family who had a ministry. Since he was "called," so were we. I owned the vision. I never felt pushed or forced into singing. I never felt used, because I was an important part of this ministry. I had a role to play, something to contribute!

I believe too often we forget about the people around us and focus all our attention on "our ministry." The people that play and sing with us on the worship team on Sunday mornings become "things" to help our ministry along, to make us look good. That's why so many people in church today begin to feel used and abused. A successful team needs a leader who will care for and look out for the interests and well-being of those he is leading.

The people who work with you need to "own the vision" in order to be truly committed and able to function as a team. "Where there is no vision, the people are unrestrained (or undisciplined), but happy is he who keeps the law" (Proverbs 29:18, NAS). Let us endeavor to share our lives with others as Jesus did with His disciples, keeping a clearly communicated vision in front of us, one that people can willingly discipline themselves for.

Impart an explicitly defined vision and purpose to those around you. "Write the vision and engrave it so plainly upon tablets that everyone who passes may [be able to] read [it easily and quickly] as he hastens by" (Habakuk 2:2, Amplified).

Just Do It!

As I walked down the hall of the "retirement center" with the other dozen or so teenagers, playing my guitar as we sang "Amazing Grace" for the 4th time, we paused outside a room for a moment and continued to sing. As I looked into the room I saw an elderly woman sitting up in bed listening with rapt attention. The glow coming from her face as she listened to the sweet refrain "I once was lost, but now am found, was blind but now I see," made it obvious she was hearing much loved words. The tears streaming down her cheeks conveyed her deep love for her Lord! As I gazed upon this woman I realized the meaning of the words of Jesus, "If you have done it unto the least of these..." We all crowded into her room and sang a hymn of her request and then had a brief prayer before continuing on down the hall. Her profuse thanks continued until we were out of sight.

As I think about those years of ministry on Sunday afternoons, I think about what Jesus had to say concerning faithfulness. Being faithful in the little things is rather a scarcity today it seems. Walking out our commitments is not always fun or easy, but Jesus said, "Well done, you upright (honorable, admirable) and faithful servant! You have been faithful and trustworthy over a little; I will put you in charge of much. Enter into and share the joy (the delight, the blessedness) which your master enjoys" (Matthew 25:21, Amplified).

Ministering in situations where there is no public glory is not easy for our flesh, but we must ask the question, "For whom are we doing it?" David spent years singing to God in front of an audience of sheep out in the pasture before he ever ministered in public before the King! He was developing a secret ministry to God!

It seems we too often take on the attitude of our society, the attitude that screams out, "This is too hard. Things are not going the way I wanted them to. I'm not getting the recognition I deserve. I'm outta here!" "...instead, whoever wants to become great among you must be your servant, and whoever wants to be first must be slave of all" (Mark 10:43-44).

I truly believe that the fruitfulness of our future ministry depends upon our faithfulness where God has placed us right now. In the midst of seeking to be faithful, remember, "Obeying the voice of the Lord is better than sacrifice" (1 Samuel 15:22b). God only requires of us what *He* asks for, not what man asks for. Bloom where God plants you!

"Whatever you do, work at it with all your heart, as working for the Lord, not for men, since you know that you will receive an inheritance from the Lord as a reward. It is the Lord Christ you are serving" (Colossians 3:23-24).

Just do it!

Jeanne Rogers

For years, Jeanne Rogers has thrilled audiences across America with powerful songs of praise and worship. Her unforgettable voice and ability to lead others in joyful worship have made her a popular ministry guest in churches and in conferences.

Since 1985, she has been praise and worship leader for the James Robison Evangelistic Association and is a featured soloist on the daily and weekly television program, "Life Today with James Robison." She has made numerous guest appearances on radio and television all across the nation. With nine solo albums and eleven live praise tapes to her credit, Jeanne was also the worship leader for the Maranatha! Music recording "Jeanne Rogers Live."

Jeanne believes that God has commissioned her to "call the people to the high mountains where they shall offer righteous sacrifices." She says, "That is an awesome responsibility and I totally lean on the Lord to carry it out."

Jeanne and her husband, Jim, live in Hurst, Texas, with their three sons.

Watch and Discern
Your Audience or Congregation

My background from early childhood was in secular entertainment. It doesn't sound too spiritual, but I brought a lot of my experience in working audiences into my worship leading. I believe God can use that training from the world if I give it to Him for "filtering." I learned as a young singer to watch my audience. I looked them in the eye and watched their response. If I wasn't communicating, I had to make the adjustment in my performance.

As a worship leader, it's easy to get your program set, and, no matter what, follow through with it because that's what you prepared. God just won't let me do that. I guess I know better from experience and training. If the congregation isn't with me, I switch gears.

My first Bible Conference in a large area of Canada brought together a cross section of denominations and fellowships. I was using local musicians, so I sent music in advance and rehearsed for two days. I did my best to plan what I felt was a conservative and familiar service for the first night. Two songs into the program, I was looking at people who were staring blankly at the words on overhead screens. I paused, cued the musicians and said, "Follow me, if you can."

"Oh, Lord, my God, when I in awesome wonder, consider all the worlds Thy hands have made... Then sings my soul, my Savior..." They were singing! No—they were worshipping! I followed that with two or three more familiar hymns and choruses to hymns. We finished and I reworked everything we'd planned for the remainder of the conference services.

I can't take credit for quick thinking in the Canadian Bible Conference. I had the coaching of a master pulpitier, not a musician. James Robison, the powerful television evangelist has been my mentor. I've been with the ministry for twenty-eight years (only about ten of those years as his worship leader). In the early days of this position, James had strong opinions about how worship was to be led, and he made those known to me before each service.

At first I was resentful and rebellious because I knew that he was not a singer or a musician. There was no blessing or anointing on my ministry while I had that attitude, so I repented. I told him I would submit and trust his strong gift of discernment. I eventually learned to discern the spirit of the group. We would talk before and after each service about what we sensed in the spirit during worship. As my discernment sharpened and I directed the service accordingly, he withdrew all input and blessed me with favor and trust.

The Lord gave me a picture of this training situation that was applied again and again. When I train my children in a new skill, I demonstrate, then I assist them with hands on. Through James, God taught me a practical lesson the same way as we teach our children.

Don McMinn

Don McMinn, Ph. D., serves on the staff of The Center for Marriage and Family Intimacy and is director of The Worship Connection. He is the author of Entering His Presence, Strategic Living, The Practice of Praise, A Heart Aflame, *and* Spiritual Strongholds.

Don has also served as worship leader at several churches in Texas and Oklahoma. Most recently he was worship leader at the 12,000-member First Baptist Church in Del City, Oklahoma.

His undergraduate degree was from the University of Texas at Austin, and he received his doctorate from North Texas State University.

Don has a particular burden to teach principles of intimacy as they relate to our relationship with God and meaningful others.

Don and his wife, Mary, have two daughters and live in the Dallas-Ft. Worth area.

Childlike Hallelujahs

My assignment: teach a third grade Sunday school class for one week.

The topic: praise.

I love to teach, so that part of the assignment was inviting. I've been a student of worship for twenty years, so I love to teach on the topic of praise. But third graders?

When the third grade Sunday school teacher asked me to teach her class about praise, I couldn't say no. After all, I had written three books on the subject and was the worship leader of our church. But I was intimidated by the challenge of having to communicate to a group of eight-year-olds. Even after thinking about it all week long, I still had no idea of how to communicate the wonders of praise and worship to fidgety children.

I was hoping the promise of Matthew 10:19 would apply to this situation: "Do not worry about what to say or how to say it. At that time you will be given what to say." And it did.

As I was walking up the stairs to the classroom, the

Lord reminded me that the night before, the L.A. Lakers and the Boston Celtics had played game seven of the NBA Finals. It was one of those classic, down-to-the-buzzer games. In the final few seconds, Boston scored the winning basket. The game was being played in the Gardens, so you can imagine the crowd's reaction during those last few moments. In the first few minutes of postgame coverage, the television commentators didn't even bother talking. The cameras scanned the audience first, then the players, and then the audience again. The activity inside the stadium said it all—Boston had won, and those who savored the victory were celebrating.

The Hebrew word "halal," (transliterated, we get the word hallelujah) means, "a spontaneous, unsolicited reaction to a joyful situation." When the Psalmist says, "Hallelujah!" he's not expressing a quiet, sober emotion. It's more similar to the emotions one would feel... at the end of a championship basketball game when one's team has just won in the final seconds.

So here's what I did when I stood in front of twenty-five third graders to teach them about praise.

After seating them on the floor, I asked how many of them had seen the championship game the night before. For the sake of those who hadn't, I retold, in great detail, the events of the last five minutes, and in particular, what went on after the game was over. After explaining the meaning of "halal," I simply drew a correlation between the feelings of joy and celebration expressed by the fans of the Boston Celtics and the joy and celebration that should erupt from our hearts whenever we think of the wonderful victory that Christ has won.

I spent a few minutes reminding the children of how awesome, wonderful, and good God is. I also reminded them of how evil, devious, and hateful Satan is. Then I took them to the cross where the battle of the ages occurred. God's best, His Son, pitted against the infamous hosts of hell. I shared with them the greatest tactical wartime strategy of all time. I described how Satan, in attempting to kill the Savior, was nothing more than a pawn manipulated by the sovereign hand of God to secure the victory of His Son. The victory was so complete that "Having disarmed the powers and authorities, He made a public spectacle of them, triumphing over them by the cross" (Colossians 2:15).

One thing I love about children is their lack of restraint, their total absence of inhibition in expressing emotion. Perhaps that's why Jesus taught us to be childlike in our faith—not childish, but childlike. Having "set up" the correlation between celebrating at a basketball game and the aura that a good praise service should have, I simply told the children that I was going to give a "countdown" from 20 to one, just like the fans do at the end of a basketball game. I told them that when I got to one, I wanted them to jump up and celebrate Jesus— because He had won the ultimate contest of the ages.

When the count was over, the children erupted into

wonderful, joyful, spontaneous, and celebrative praise. They yelled, clapped, jumped up and down, and hugged each other. It was a sight to behold. God inhabited the praise of those children and those few moments became for me an unforgettable experience.

Yes, a lesson on praise was taught that day, and I was one of the students.

Praise is simply acknowledging, honoring, and celebrating the person and work of Christ. In colloquial terms, praise is just bragging on Jesus.

My prayer is that God will grant me a boldness to unashamedly declare His great worth, both in the "sanctuary" and as a lifestyle. I pray for a child-likeness in my worship; that I'll be so caught up in the wonder of His majesty and grace that I won't worry about what others around me are or are not doing or what they're thinking about me as I express my love to God.

God, give us hearts to worship You in a great child-like way.

John Wyatt

John Wyatt graduated from Baylor University in 1994 with a bachelor's degree in church music. He did graduate study at North Texas State University in music education and post-graduate work in management at the University of Texas in Austin.

John has served a number of Southern Baptist churches and spent seven years traveling with Fulness Ministries of Fort Worth, Texas, as a worship leader and seminar speaker. He has written several articles for Christian magazines on the subject of praise and worship.

Currently, John serves as associate pastor of music and worship at the 7,000-member Casas Adobes Baptist Church in Tucson, Arizona. Each week he coordinates and leads the worship leadership teams for a Saturday evening worship service and three Sunday morning worship services. The church has a 125-voice choir and a 35-piece orchestra. There are also a number of other vocal and instrumental

ensembles who share the leadership responsibilities.
John and his wife, Judy, live in Tucson.

How Many Songs Can a Church Sing?

When I first came to our church someone made the comment, "We keep singing the same old songs over and over again." I have to admit I thought that was a problem and that it was my job to fix it. So, I started teaching new songs.

After a year or so I began to notice the people weren't singing as confidently as they used to. The sense of intensity was missing from our worship. At first I didn't know what was wrong. Eventually, I realized that in trying to keep from singing the same few songs over and over, I had introduced too many songs and we weren't singing them often enough. While trying to get the church out of the ditch on one side of the road, I had run it off in the ditch on the other side. In one ditch the people acted bored and uninspired. In the other, they struggled with songs they didn't know very well.

It's my job to do things that help people worship God with zest and abandonment. There is no zest when you feel bored, and there is no abandonment when you feel uncertain. I needed help. The solution was a well-balanced master song list. Here are some thoughts I have found helpful in putting together our list.

Most of the songs are "fresh songs." Fresh songs are those songs that are neither old or new. People love to sing them and they sing them with enthusiasm. A fresh song still "catches fire" when it is sung. These songs help bring excitement and energy during the worship time. They are songs that have not been used so much that they are worn out.

Some of the songs should be "old songs." These are songs that were our favorites before we wore them out. They are still effective if used sparingly. I think it's good to use an "old song" in just about every service.

A few of the songs should be brand new, the best new songs you can find. By definition, these are simply songs we have not used at our church. Trial and error have convinced me it's wise to include no more than one new or recently introduced song in any given service.

We also include hymns regularly in our services. Often we take old hymns and put a new groove under them. Just today, one of our senior citizens mentioned to me that she liked the way the new rhythms freshen up the old hymns. She also told me that she'd been telling a friend of her's about the new rhythmic patterns we are using to accompany the hymns. The lady had remarked, "You know, I didn't know what they were doing to the hymns, but I sure like it."

The worship at our church has benefitted significantly as we have implemented a carefully conceived master song list. This concept has done two things. It has insured freshness; when the songs are fresh, people want to sing them. It has also insured familiarity; when the songs are familiar, the people are able to sing them. These two things have happened because our list contains the right number of songs and it contains the right proportion of fresh songs, new songs and old songs. The result: a worship service where the singing is challenging, uplifting, stimulating and at the same time accessible to the majority of the people. The singing gets powerful. The worship gets intense. God comes!

David Ritter

David Ritter is a graduate of Northwest College of the Assemblies of God. He has been a minister of music for 18 years and is currently serving at Phoenix First Assembly in Phoenix, Arizona, with Pastor Tommy Barnett.

David is recognized nationally for his songwriting, arranging, orchestrating, producing and worship leading, with several songs of his having been released by major publishers. He also had the privilege of being the worship leader on the Integrity's Hosanna! Music recording "All Hail the Power." David is sought after as a teacher and keynote speaker at praise and worship seminars, choir retreats, and pastoral conventions across the nation.

David feels his greatest gift has been his wife, Grace, and their three children.

God Causes Praise to Arise

About four years ago an angel of the Lord appeared to me in a dream and said that he had a message for me from the Lord. I remember the incredible excitement and anticipation. He had my full attention! "God is displeased with your self-activist attitude." I sat there (stunned) not knowing what he meant. I said, "Could you explain?"

"You have taken the credit for leading people into worship. You have not activated or created worship experiences by the way you lead choruses, or the songs you've written, or your orchestrated choruses, or your choir or your voice. It is the Spirit of God that moves within the hearts of believers, prodding them to respond with praise. God has used you as a prompter because you have been open to Him." I asked him for a Scripture to confirm this and he said, "Isaiah 43:20-21."

Immediately I awakened (shaking from the presence of the Lord) and opened my Bible to Isaiah 43:20-21. "...because I give waters in the wilderness, and rivers in the desert, to give drink to My people, My chosen. This people have I formed for myself; they shall show forth My praise."

What an incredible release! It finally dawned on me that God gives the reason to praise. I had been guilty of playing "cheerleader" to get people to worship God. I had also found myself using public response as a gauge for the effectiveness and credibility of my ministry. I had fallen in to the great misconception that I was responsible for leading people to God!

Through this dream I saw that we as worshippers have been called to do only one simple thing—worship God. God does not ask us to go out and make people respond. He just asks us to be obedient and open. Nowhere in Scripture does God say, "You must make people praise Me; if you don't get them to respond, then you have failed the Lord thy God!" God does tell us however, to sing "psalms, hymns, spiritual songs," and "new songs." He also tells us to "worship God with all of your heart and soul and mind and strength" (Mark 12:30). What He doesn't say is, "Do whatever gimmicks and special effects you can muster up to get others to respond."

In attempting to evaluate the dream, I pondered why God would send a angel to tell me I had an attitude problem when I have committed sins which I feel have been much more serious. I felt the Lord gently speaking to my heart that He is not as concerned about our actions as He is with the motives behind them. The attitude of the heart is what matters to God. This should encourage us to keep our hearts right so that when we do stumble, we can know God's constant forgiveness *in spite of ourselves.* Come boldly before the throne!

Bob Kauflin

After receiving a piano performance degree from Temple University in 1976, Bob Kauflin traveled for eight years with the contemporary Christian group, Glad, as a writer, speaker and arranger. In 1984 he left the group to pursue involvement in the local church. Although he continues to write for Glad, his growing passion since that time has been worship. Bob was the worship leader on "Chosen Treasure" from Integrity's Hosanna! Music and has produced three worship albums for churches related through People of Destiny International.

Bob and his wife, Julie, and their six children live in Charlotte, North Carolina, where he serves as an associate pastor for Abundant Life Community Church.

Happy Birthday to You

The song of the Lord, or prophetic singing, is an area of worship that has intrigued me ever since I learned of its existence about ten years ago. By "song of the Lord" I'm referring especially to spontaneous songs which reflect God's heart toward His people or spontaneous songs which are sung corporately to God.

One of the more memorable songs the Lord gave me was during a worship group rehearsal years ago. We had been focusing on the sovereign rule of Jesus, and I was overwhelmed with the thought of Jesus having the name above all names and being so worthy of our worship. In the midst of our worship, I began singing, "You have been given the name above all names and we worship You, yes we worship You." Gradually the group picked it up, and we had a wonderful time worshipping together with a spontaneous song. After that, I was open to singing spontaneously during worship as I felt led. However, I failed to step out consistently due to doubts about my motives. "Why do I want to do this? Do I want to make a good impression on everyone? What if I go blank in the middle of a phrase? What if my song has no effect on anyone?" Accusations and discouraging thoughts generally kept me quiet, except for the rare occasion when I had a very strong impression.

In 1992, while at a leaders' conference, God graciously broke through my dull heart with the truth that my duty was simply to obey His voice, not to predict the effect of my prophetic song or to second-guess my motives. God showed me that my heart would never be *entirely* pure, so I could be released to obey His voice, while trusting Him to expose and change any wrong motives. I experienced a release of prophetic songs almost immediately. What a relief to know that God Himself was responsible for not only the impression but the fruit as well.

Later that year, this lesson was driven home at another conference in Indiana, Pennsylvania. About 3000 men, women, and children had gathered from different churches related through People of Destiny International, led by C.J. Mahaney, for a weekend of worship, ministry, and teaching. During one of the last worship sessions, C.J. came up to the microphone to apologetically explain how he had been struggling all weekend with a word he felt the Lord had wanted him to share. He acknowledged that he had to give it, no matter how foolish it might seem. "I'd like everyone whose birthday is in May to please stand up. I believe the Lord wants to minister to you." In the next moments, I distinctly felt the Lord was giving me a song for those who were standing. Everything seemed fine and under control until I thought God was telling me that the climax of the song was going to be the words, "So happy birthday to you, happy birthday, my chosen ones, I have loved you for all time." I remember thinking, "If I go through with this either the heavens are going to open or my friends will never let me live this down." With fear and trepidation, I forged ahead. Regardless of the consequences, I knew I had to obey what I thought to be the voice of the Lord.

Reports came back in the following weeks of how God had ministered to various people through that prophetic song. One woman had been adopted as a child and had never been able to forgive her parents for abandoning her. For the first time God broke through her unforgiveness in a tangible way and she felt His love wash away her sense of rejection and feeling forsaken. A pastor related that it was one of the most significant times of ministry he had experienced. Many of those standing wept as God's love was freshly shed abroad in their hearts. Had these people been affected through some brilliant, finely crafted spontaneous song, I might have tried to take some credit. But what touched their hearts and broke down their defenses was someone singing "happy birthday." I learned then, as I continue to learn, that God is not impressed with my gifts or abilities. He gave them to me. What He is interested in is my humility leading to obedience. My protests not withstanding, if

God can use Balaam's donkey, He can use me to speak to others. The question is not how profound or unique my words are, but how faithful I am to speak or sing them when God gives them to me.

Graham Kendrick

Graham Kendrick's songs and hymns are sung by millions of people in numerous languages around the world. Some of his best known songs include, "Shine, Jesus, Shine," "Rejoice, Rejoice, Christ is in You," and "Amazing Love." He is a co-founder of March for Jesus which went global in 1994 with about 10 million people participating.

A self-taught guitarist, Graham began writing and performing his songs during his teenage years, and, after training as a teacher, ventured out full-time in music at the age of 22.

He and his wife, Jill, have four daughters and live in South London.

Lord, I'm Empty...

In Psalm 103 the psalmist applies his will to stir his whole being. "Praise the Lord, O my soul; all that is within my inmost being, praise His holy name. Praise the Lord, O my soul, and forget not all His benefits." He is talking to himself, stirring himself into action. He is, as it were, shaking himself by his own lapels, picking himself up out of his own slumber and or apathy, and demanding obedience of all his faculties. The discipline of worship requires that we stand in complete readiness for obedience to the Spirit, like a soldier preparing himself for action.

I remember clearly an occasion on which this lesson was firmly printed on my mind. I had been invited to lead worship at a church some hours drive away from home, so my wife and I set off early that morning in the rather ramshackle Morris 1000 van we had at the time. The weather was cold and icy, and the wind blew freely through the many gaps and holes in the vehicle!

I was in a grumpy mood and proceeded reluctantly, creating tension between my wife and me. At the time, I was spiritually dry and had no desire or motivation to travel such a long way, let alone to lead worship! By the time we arrived, my mood was blacker, the tension tauter, and the temperature colder.

For the duration of the last five minutes prior to facing the crowd of enthusiastic would-be praisers, I knew I faced a stark choice: Would I get right with the Lord, my wife (and the car!) and go on in raw faith, or be honest with my hosts and back out?

Probably motivated at least in part by pride, I decided on the former course of action. I confessed my sin, apologized to my wife and stepped into the meeting saying to the Lord something to the effect of, "Lord, I'm empty. I don't feel like worshipping You. I have nothing to give to You or with which to lead the people unless You give it to me. But, sink or swim, here I go!"

From the moment I began to lead the praise, my heart filled up and we praised with freedom and joy. I did not have to pretend or put on an act. Because I had determined to praise, the Lord ignited praise within me, and I genuinely overflowed.

At times I would like to forget that lesson. Usually those times are when I am not leading but instead am part of the congregation and feeling similarly fed up and grumpy. I would like to use my mood as a legitimate excuse not to join in, but (to the irritation of the less noble side of me) I now know that my feelings need not rule my spirit.

Excerpted from *Learning to Worship as a Way of Life,*© 1984 Graham Kendrick. Published in the United States by Bethany House Publishers, Minneapolis, Minnesota. Used by permission.

Joel Ragains

Joel Ragains has been the worship pastor at Graceland Baptist Church in New Albany, Indiana, for the past 27(!) years. Graceland is part of the Southern Baptist convention with an average weekly attendance of 2,200. Joel is in charge of eight worship teams as well as a 100-voice choir. Joel sees one of his main responsibilities as discipling others in leading worship and has fulfilled this call through Graceland's numerous satellite churches. He is a graduate of Southwest Baptist University in Bolivar, Missouri, and Southern Baptist Theological Seminary in Louisville, Kentucky.

An avid gardener, Joel and his wife, Mary Ellen, have two children and two grand children and reside in New Albany, Indiana.

The Revival of 1980

In the late 1970s the church that I have now served in for the past 27 years began to pray for a revival. As we neared the end of that decade, it appeared on the surface as though the more we prayed the less likely revival was to come. We had a traditional Southern Baptist church, and we followed the normal worship format of a couple of hymns, a choir special, preaching, and the invitation ("Just As I Am"). Then we went home.

Having just moved to a new church building, the staff and people were stressed out, tired and discouraged. In the midst of that situation our pastor had a heart attack and was counseled by his physicians that he should retire because of the extensive damage to his heart. He and his wife got away. While they were gone, God spoke to him and said He was going to heal him. The pastor came back to our church and shared that testimony. Needless to say, it began to shake our foundation and created a real desire in me to explore other forms of worship leading.

The beginning of a new decade brought a change to

our church, my life, and other lives that has forever changed the course of our ministry. We invited a pastor from Ft. Worth, Texas, to come and lead a four-day Bible conference in May of 1980. Little did we know that God would sovereignly move among us and extend that four-day conference to an 18-week meeting with Him.

Out of that meeting I began to realize the importance of praise and worship when the corporate body gathers together. My formal training was to be a minister of music which enabled me to administer a graded choir program. I did not know what a worship leader was, but I knew that God was putting in me a desire to lead His people into His presence. Up until the revival of 1980 my ministry had focused on singing about Jesus. After that meeting I began to sing to the Lord—a whole new approach for me. That was nearly 15 years ago. This one experience continues to shape and direct my worship leading today.

When I began to break out of my traditional mold, members of the congregation began to express their concerns about the new freedom that was coming in our services. Some of the concerns were given verbally and some were in the form of passive resistance through body language and minimal participation in the worship service. Because of my longevity with the church, many of the members were very close to both me and my family. As I looked out and saw these people they were more than nameless faces—they were people involved with me in ministry. Consequently, I was forced to develop an attitude of receiving them as they were.

There were some of the choir members who felt that more expressive worship was not for them. They held to the model of two hymns, a choir special and then the message (sermon). It was difficult for them to see themselves as worshippers first and singers second. So, I kept the choir program intact, but used the first 30 minutes of Thursday-evening rehearsals as a teaching time. I started a laboratory for integrating new styles of worship into our church body. Making these gradual changes has had a powerful impact in modeling worship to our congregation.

Then the time came to promote, from the pulpit, an attitude of receiving each other. So stepping forward, I made exhortations like: "We are here to worship the Lord; everyone doesn't have to worship alike," "Your garment of praise may not be like mine; and that's okay," or "Just worship as you feel appropriate for you." This approach really helped to disarm some of the criticism.

Learning to deal with criticism has been good as well as painful. One difficult part was being critiqued by fellow members of our church pastoral team. Each pastor is gifted in different ways, and we don't worship alike. These differences have produced a lot a thinking-through and soul-searching. I have stretched the others and in turn they have stretched me. Remember, if you receive constructive criticism it can help you to rethink what and why you are doing what you're doing and bring balance.

Criticism even came from my own family. My wife and children had become comfortable with what I was before the transition from minister of music to worship pastor. My wife, who has always been supportive, was finding herself vulnerable and uncomfortable in the new style of worship and with my role as worship leader. The key ingredient in helping my wife and children learn to be worshippers was not by modeling it in the public, but by teaching them at home the biblical reasons for freedom in worship and encouraging them to be open to pursue these freedoms. This took commitment on my part to accept the responsibility to be the priest in my home.

In the midst of these changes the Lord opened my eyes to the following verses.

"And in that day shall ye say, Praise the Lord, call upon His name, declare His doings among the people, make mention that His name is exalted. Sing unto the Lord; for He hath done excellent things: this is known in all the earth. Cry out and shout, thou inhabitants of Zion: for great is the Holy One of Israel in the midst of thee" (Isaiah 12:4-6).

I am committed to doing just that.

Rev. Clayton Brasington, III

Rev. Clay Brasington has been serving as an ordained minister of music for 20 years. He holds a master's degree in church music from Southern Baptist Theological Seminary, as well as a bachelor's degree in music education from Florida State University. When he was a young man in junior high school, he responded publicly to God's unmistakable call to full-time ministry.

Clay is currently the worship leader for a new contemporary worship service at Coral Ridge Presbyterian Church in Fort Lauderdale, Florida. He has been sharing the gospel through contemporary music for 15 years and desires to see worship become more than a spectator sport. Clay's consistent prayer is that believers gather with a hunger to participate in worshipping God.

Clay and his wife, Dee, have been married for 25 years. Together they formulated and began teaching the Marriage and Family Life Seminars in churches 15 years ago, and this ministry is ongoing today. Clay and Dee have three children and have had several foster children. Clay also serves as a police chaplain.

I Don't Need You

I came to Christ at the age of seven. I was fourteen when I responded publicly to God's call to the ministry. It seems as though I've known most of my life that this was God's purpose and plan for me. I was especially drawn to the music ministry, and after six years of formal graduate education, I began pursuing the vision full-time. However, after seven years of leading church worship services, choirs, youth groups, etc., I felt as though I was continually pouring water into a leaky bucket. No matter how hard I worked to pump it up, my efforts in ministry seemed to bring only temporary results. I was frustrated and on my way to becoming a confirmed workaholic. I began to ask, "God, is this all there is?" I had no idea that I was about to have an encounter with God that would forever change my life and ministry.

I went to bed one evening feeling fine, but awoke in

the middle of the night in excruciating pain. It was absolutely electrifying and incapacitating. I felt as though my sternum and every major joint in my body had been shattered. Over the next few weeks, numerous doctors conducted extensive testing on my body, but they could not determine my illness. They just felt it was extremely serious. I spent two months bedridden under doctor's orders and left home only to undergo more tests.

Many saints offered up prayers on my behalf. I was anointed with oil by the elders of my church, and my family and I prayed—all seemingly to no avail. I felt as though the heavens were brass, and my faith began to reach an all-time low. I not only questioned why God would not heal me, but I even came to the point that I was tempted to doubt His very existence. My frustration and pain sent me again and again to the Word and to prayer. After two months, I emerged from the inner battle with confidence that God was real and that His Word was Truth. But the intensity of the pain never lessened. The doctor's reports remained grim, and I was convinced that I might die soon, so I wrote a personal letter to each of my children, encouraging them to stand for God regardless of any circumstances they may face in life.

But I was angry with God, and I finally cried out to Him in desperation. With shameless arrogance, I told Him that He was being unfair and that He should feel lucky to have me on His team. I reminded Him of all the good things I was doing for Him... I shouldn't be treated this way! He needed me! I demanded answers now. My attitude was shameless and disrespectful... but finally *honest*.

What happened next shook me to the core of my being. I heard God speak so clearly—whether with my ears or my spirit, I am uncertain. But He said, "Clay, I've seen all the things you have been doing, and they are good things. The only problem is that *I am not in them*. You are doing it all yourself. And furthermore, Clay, *I don't need you*." I was devastated. I cried out again to God; but this time it was a cry like Isaiah's, "Woe is me, for I am undone." I wept before the Lord in repentance and asked forgiveness for my arrogance and fleshly attempts to do spiritual things.

Assuming that God had given me the last chance to confess my sins before dying, I received assurance of His forgiveness and cleansing and then committed my family into His care... and waited to die. But nothing happened. Truthfully, I was a bit disappointed. I had grown so weary of pain that death would have seemed a welcome relief. But since I was still living, I promised God that I would strive never again to minister "in the flesh." I yielded myself to do whatever He asked of me, small or large. "Just tell me what you want me to do, Lord," I pled. His response was, "*I want you to praise Me*." Being the fast learner that I am, I said, "But God, I can't do that; it hurts too much to breathe, much less to sing!" Silence. So I dragged myself to the piano and began to make up songs, trying to praise God for how I felt. It was pitiful, and after a few minutes I stopped and said, "Lord, I've just come clean with You, and now I'm being dishonest again. There's no way that I can, with any integrity, praise You for how I feel. I'm really hurting. Have You ever hurt like this?" What a stupid question. While the words were still on my lips, I envisioned Jesus hanging on the cross. Again I asked forgiveness, and said, "Just what am I supposed to praise You for? I may lose my job soon. Our home belongs to the church. I'm unemployable, and I'm probably about to die."

Again, God spoke so clearly to me. (His mercy endures forever!) He said, *"I am the Alpha and the Omega, the Beginning and the End. You worship Me for who I am, for I never change."* I was filled with the awe of His presence. As I began to sing songs about the greatness of God and His character, I began to understand firsthand what it meant to *worship God in spirit and in truth.* Nearly an hour later, I stood up from the piano. As I stood, the pain seemed to shatter and fall from me, beginning at the top of my head and continuing down to the soles of my feet. God healed me. This Southern Baptist began to dance and leap for joy before the Lord!

This glorious encounter with God took place fifteen years ago, but I remember it as though it were yesterday. The principles for ministry and worship have been so burned into my heart that they act as a "cattle prod" anytime I begin to stray from the truths born out of adversity.

These principles which guide my personal walk with Christ as well are:

1. God is faithful to perform His Word, and is not slow about His promise as some count slowness. He will perform it.

2. God doesn't need me as a servant, but He genuinely longs to have intimate fellowship with me. This is a prerequisite to my knowing how He wants me to serve Him.

3. Pride may be subtle to its owner but is deeply destructive and will strangle the flow of God's Spirit and blessings.

4. We are to praise God in everything...not necessarily for everything. Our focus needs to be on Him who never changes, not on the circumstances. God's character is immutable.

5. We are to sing to the Lord, rather than just about Him. Almighty God is the object of our worship, and He is our audience (not the congregation or those around us).

6. I cannot outdo God. Whenever I minister to the Lord, He ministers back to me.

Lynn DeShazo

Lynn DeShazo is a gifted worship leader and the author of numerous songs, many of which have appeared on Integrity's Hosanna! Music recordings. Lynn is presently an exclusive songwriter for Integrity Music and is best known for such songs as "More Precious Than Silver," "Lead Me to the Rock," "You Have Called Us," "Turn My Heart," and "Be Magnified."

Lynn resides in her hometown, Birmingham, Alabama. When she is not on the road as part of her traveling ministry she serves as worship leader and musician at Liberty Church.

My Pastor, My Encourager

I remember very distinctly the day my pastor asked me to take over the worship leading responsibilities for our small fellowship in Ann Arbor, Michigan. The request came as a surprise to me even though I had been a part of our worship team since the inception of the church three years earlier. Our current worship leader, an excellent musician, would soon be leaving and the "mantle" was being passed to me.

I replied, "Well... okay, Mike, but I'd be happy just to play guitar while you lead, if you'd rather do it that way." Interpretation: "I'm not so sure about this. Wouldn't you like to be a worship leading pastor?!"

The truth was, I probably would have been quite content just playing along with the worship team, at least for a while. I was quite comfortable in the familiar role of a supporting (i.e. not in charge) team member.

Pastor Mike, however, was undaunted by my hesitance. "Lynn, you've got an anointing on your life to lead worship. I know you can do this!" He assured me I was suited for the task and that we would work together as a team until the transition was made successfully. Pastor Mike Caulk and I put our heads together on song lists for worship services and practiced with the rest of the worship team on Saturdays. On Sunday mornings, he'd call the congregation to worship and lead us in heartily-sung praise medleys, often interspersed with exhortations. I'd play along, leading the other musicians and helping us all to make the transitions between songs.

We hit our share of snags, of course. Sometimes Mike's exhortations turned into mini-sermons and we'd lose "the flow." Sometimes I'd miss his cues to go on to the next song and we sounded like a train wreck. Occasionally, Mike would lean over and whisper, "How do we end this song?" and I'd try to keep from breaking up in laughter.

All in all, our approach worked out pretty well, though. The Lord was praised, we had fun, and my confidence grew. The day eventually came when Mike stepped down from his interim role as worship leader and turned that responsibility completely over to me.

A true pastor wants to see each one of the sheep entrusted to his care grow into a mature believer. He recognizes that God never intended him to do everything himself (even when it seems easier that way), but to train and disciple the church to do the work of ministry with increasing effectiveness.

Perhaps the most important feat accomplished in that transitional period was the growing of my confidence.

My pastor prodded me in a direction I needed to step out in and then wisely gave me all the practical support he was capable of until I could lead a worship service on my own. I don't remember that day as clearly as the other one, but I must have done alright because I kept the job for the next five years. Leading God's people in worship continues to be a prime area of ministry for me.

Dennis Jernigan

Dennis Jernigan is a worship leader who believes his calling in life is to lead others into a heart-to-heart confrontation with the Lord Jesus Christ through his music. He endeavors to bring others to the realization that "God is here. He loves us. We need Him. Now deal with it!"

Born and raised on a small Oklahoma farm near the town of Boynton, Dennis was reared in the Southern Baptist faith. He discovered at an early age that he had a very special gift from the Lord—he could hear music then reproduce what he heard at the piano. By the time he was nine years old, Dennis was regularly playing the piano during worship at First Baptist Church in Boynton.

Dennis feels his calling is to bring the message of hope and healing through the worship of Almighty God to the Body of Christ. In fact, his heart's desire is to see the whole Body of Christ come together in worship, regardless of denominational affiliation. In 1993, Dennis stepped down from his staff position in Oklahoma City, moved his family back to the farm where he was raised, and now regularly shares his music and message of intimacy with God across the nation.

Many of Dennis' worship recordings, including his latest, "I Will Trust You," are available on the HeartCry label.

Dennis married Melinda Hewlitt in 1983 and they are the proud parents of nine(!) children. They presently make their home (in the words of one friend) past country on the farm where Dennis grew up.

The Making of a Worship Leader

As I look back over my life and admit where I have failed, it becomes easier to see how knowledge of the truth has set me free. Who I am, my identity, as a worshiper and as a worship leader has been shaped by the truths as well as by the lies I have believed.

I was raised in the Southern Baptist denomination. From the time I was nine years old I was the church pianist. Because I felt I had to perform for my father's acceptance and approval, I also felt this was the way I must respond to God: to "do right" so He would love me.

Another contributing factor in my journey toward finding my identity was the fact that I struggled with my sexual identity—with homosexuality—from my earliest memories. Because I saw how the church responded to this particular sin (not in love), my heart was bound in a prison of fears and lies. This only helped feed my need to perform. I had to be the best at everything so everyone would like me. I started on the basketball team in each year of high school. I was valedictorian of my senior class (of thirteen!). I led out in school and church activities and anything else that could bolster my self-esteem. Going away to college left me alone and open to an ever-deepening cycle of sin and performance that never seemed to satisfy, and I began to wonder if intimacy with God was really possible.

After graduation from a well-known Southern Baptist university with not a clue as to my purpose in life, I had come to the bottom of my heart's well concerning my personal struggle with homosexuality and my identity. I was basically ready to give up on life, and, subsequently, on God. Fortunately, God saw fit to give me some time off for the purpose of dealing with these issues. You may be wondering, "What in the world does this have to do with leading worship?" That is a valid question. But in my estimation, this was the beginning of a ministry for which I had no personal aspirations, one of which I had no concept—the ministry of leading others into intimacy with the Father.

If you have worked toward a music degree or know someone who has, you will understand this glimpse of God's sense of humor. God moved me to live with a family in Oklahoma City. The only job I could get was that of a school bus driver! While this seemed desperate to me at first, I soon came to realize God's wisdom. I had an early morning route and an afternoon route, with several hours to kill in between. Because I had no clues as to my identity and because I had no one else to teach me, I simply put my Bible on the piano during those in-between hours, turned to the Psalms, and did what David did. I simply got honest with God.

In the mornings, I actually had two bus routes with 25 minutes between those routes. During those 25 minutes, I would park my bus in an abandoned housing addition and write in my journal. This journal was the method I found most helpful in getting my deepest, darkest, and most intimate thoughts—about anything—out in the open to God. Day in and day out I wrote of hurts, disillusionments, failures, emotions, and any other soul-data I found needing to come out. What I discovered in the process was that God really was concerned with my feelings, whatever they might be, and however dark they may seem to me. I found God approachable and desirous of *my* presence. In fact, I began to understand that God took more delight in my presence than I could possibly take in His! After that first year of keeping a journal, I felt God impress me to burn it. Page by page I burned my deepest heart-cries and most horrendous secrets. Gently and tenderly, Father God taught me that just as this picture of my past was being burned away, so too, He had cleansed me of my past—and present and future—and forever forgave and forgot the wickedness of my heart.

I continued to cry out to Him from the piano day by day, many times literally in tears because I had tried to live for God so many times in the past only to fall deeper and deeper into the trenches of sin. My concept of God was that of a cosmic policeman—a distant God waiting for me to mess up so He could step back into my life and bop me on the head. I felt ashamed and unworthy of His love. I felt that God was unapproachable. Still, I could not yet give up.

Day by day, as I cried out to God, I began doing what I saw David had done. Not only did I become bluntly honest with my God, I also began to write down my prayers, which, for me, happened to come out in the form of songs! Soon, I came to realize that God's love for me was not based on how well I performed in this life but upon my recognition of His abiding presence in my life, no matter how deeply in sin I had fallen, and no matter how inconsistent I was in my love for Him. My heart was broken when I realized there was nothing I could do to earn His love, because He loved me no matter what!

This truth was brought to the forefront of my heart through the ministry of *The Second Chapter of Acts*. During one of their concerts, Annie Herring shared that God had shown her there was someone present who carried something so shameful in their heart that they would be devastated if they thought anyone knew about it. She shared that God knew—and that He loved that person anyway. I knew that someone was me. By faith, I lifted my sin to Jesus and told Him I could not overcome it, but that I would let Him carry it away for me. As *Second Chapter* sang "Mansion Builder," I saw my sin placed upon Christ, myself crucified and buried with Him and my sin. And I saw Him risen and calling me to come forth and be someone brand new! That night, the power of that sin was broken in my life, and the worship and songs began to pour out like a river!

As the songs began to flow, I began to look for others to sing them to and to sing them with. I soon realized that if I simply entered boldly into His presence, it did not matter if others followed me. Two things quickly became apparent to me. First, I realized that my job was simply to seek God's heart. Second, I understood that the Good Shepherd never beat His sheep or forced them to worship Him. As I became more and more free in my expression to Him, others seemed to be drawn to Him *with* me.

Around this time, another godly family had taken me under their wings. They began to encourage me to worship God in ways this Southern Baptist boy had only heard about. What I found was that God had given me a body to use in expressing my heart. He gave me emotions with which to express my feelings. And above all else, He showed me that He was worthy of all my love, because He had literally born all my sins on the cross.

As I began writing down my prayers, it became a very natural progression to share those songs with my friends. It was quite overwhelming when they seemed to take the songs and sing them as their own. It was during many nights around the piano that I first learned to express my heart in openness and honesty to the Lord in a corporate setting. It was also here that I began to realize that a person's response to God was not my responsibility. It is each person's choice. I realized that I need not try to coerce anyone to praise God.

A few short years later, I found myself working as a church janitor/secretary. One Sunday, the music minister said God had shown him he was standing in the wrong place and that Dennis Jernigan was to be leading the worship. That very day I led worship for the first time for a large group of people and found my calling in life—to help others know Jesus Christ in an intimate and deep way through worship.

Just as God so faithfully met with me in my first feeble and awkward attempts at communing with Him, He has been faithful to lead me deeper and deeper into an ever-growing, vibrant, living relationship with a living God. The one thing I would share with anyone concerning leading worship is this: seek God for yourself. Seek Him and not a ministry. Find Him and ministry will come as a natural overflow of the life lived seeking Him. He will be as near as we need Him to be.

In leading others to worship Him I simply seek Him myself and encourage those who desire to meet with Him to go with me. I don't worry whether they follow or not. The way I see it, just as God was so faithful to meet me where I was, He can do the same for anyone else who genuinely recognizes their need and then sets out to seek Him in whatever way they know.

Why do I worship? I cannot help myself. I see where I would be had it not been for Jesus Christ. Worship begins in the heart. Anything outward is simply an extension of what's on the inside. At best, we see through a glass dimly. And, yes, one day we will see Him face to face.

The following helps explain my definition of a worshiper and of a worship leader:

Here is my heart, Lord. Wipe off as much of the grime and dust that separates me from You as You can in this life so there is no big change when I finally step into eternity. A life lived with the heart exposed to the Light is the life of a worshiper. And this truly is a worship leader—one who shares that heart and lives out that heart before others.

David Grothe

David Grothe is the minister of music at Victory Christian Center in Tulsa, Oklahoma. Along with pastoral duties, David directs all the musical outreaches of the church. A native Tulsan, David received his undergraduate degree in music education from Oral Roberts University and is continuing graduate studies in church music. Full-time ministry began with three and half years of ministry with the ORU World Action Teams in national crusades, as well as the weekly Oral Roberts television programs. David worked for three years with the music department at Rhema Bible Training Center as staff arranger and music instructor. While at Rhema he taught music ministry courses and traveled extensively, leading worship in the Kenneth Hagin crusades and camp meetings.

As a studio musician, David has sung, played and led worship for numerous recordings including Integrity Hosanna! Music's "Arise and Sing." David and his wife, Becky, have four children.

Loving People, Serving Leaders

I suppose I've always seen worship leading as an act of leading and loving people.

At nine years old I began to attend a church where a man named Vep Ellis, Jr., was the minister of music. Vep came from a rich heritage of gospel music, having traveled and sung in camp meetings and churches with his family all of his life. His life and ministry at our church made a great impression on my life. As a young boy, my answer to the question, "What do you want to do when you grow up?" was, "I want to do what Vep does!"

Many times I've thought about what it was that made such an impact on my life. There was wonderful singing, great playing, and a super-joyful noise being offered to the Lord. But the thing that really marked me for life was the love he showed people. A personal interest in individuals, as well as the whole body of believers, was so important to Vep.

I learned some foundational truths about music and worship as a young person in the church music program, but the most important thing I learned was how to relate to people and minister to their needs. I learned that the minister of music must be as much a *minister* as he is a *musician*. For instance, if I was in the church choir or playing in the praise band, I had to be ready to pray with someone at the altar during times of ministry. Vep taught me that hospital calls, home visits and personal counseling were as much a part of our ministry in music as anything else.

It all goes along with what 1 Peter 5:1-3 says about "feeding the flock of God which is among you." I see leading worship in the pastoral light of loving people and helping them draw close to God. That's when He draws close to us.

Since I began leading worship in college, I have learned another principle as I have regularly had the opportunity to lead in a variety of situations—in many different places, using different styles of music, and among different types of people. One thing has always stayed the same, however. It has been necessary for me to flow with the leadership that asked me (or appointed me) to lead that part of the meeting. This has been apparent wherever I have been, whether at a home prayer meeting, an outdoor evangelistic crusade, a businessman's dinner, a large Christian conference, a teaching seminar, a Sunday morning church service, or an overseas missions outreach. I have had to realize that as a worship leader I'm a man under authority.

Our success is based upon our willingness to find out what is needed or expected for that particular service and do it with a willing heart. Sometimes a long and extended time of just waiting on the Lord is the order of the day, but in another meeting a couple of opening songs is all that is needed. I've learned that when I'm appointed to do a certain task (i.e. lead worship) in a particular meeting, it's not my place to impose my desires or plans. I am to flow with the desire of the leadership. It's often a hard thing to put the flesh under and go with the flow, but that's where the real blessing of God is on our lives.

I am not suggesting you compromise what you believe about praise and worship. I am suggesting you find the wonderful place of submission and humility and be a servant wherever you find yourself. You will begin to see that worship leading is really just a matter of leading, serving and loving people.

David
Garratt

David Garratt, along with his wife Dale, pioneered Scripture in Song praise and worship music. For the past 27 years David has been involved in recording and publishing praise and worship songs, as well as teaching and leading many of God's people in worship throughout many parts of the world.

Currently David is working with a number of indigenous groups encouraging them to offer the treasures from their cultures to God.

David and Dale reside in New Zealand.

Drapes, Pews and a
Dancing Worship Leader

By 1982, after almost 10 years of ministering in praise and worship and 14 years after recording our first praise and worship tape, we were in some ways considered experts in a field that until then few others seemed to be a part of.

Dale and I had travelled to Europe, America, Asia and Africa as well as around Australia and New Zealand, which are our home territories. We had led and taught in these places and felt we had some understanding of at least the basics.

Then, early in 1982, two men, one a Welshman and the other from Arkansas in the United States, visited New Zealand to do some teaching on prophecy and worship. We travelled as part of the ministering team, leading worship in various locations around the nation.

The problem was that the American was teaching on being free to "dance before the Lord." Not the sort of dance that's done by people skilled in creative movement but the sort that the newly crowned King David did before the Lord, leaping for joy in an unrestrained way.

This teaching shattered my status-quo to say the least! It challenged my spiritual equilibrium, broke into my neatly constructed boxes of what was proper and what wasn't. Worst of all I knew I heard God saying, "Unless you become like a little child you won't even enter..."

At that time Dale and I were leading a group of worshippers at a local "mainline" church, and the things we were doing were considered radical enough *without this*! However, God helped us, and over the following months, at our Tuesday evening praise times at the local school auditorium, we found ourselves becoming free in spontaneous praise. These times even included expressions of dance. The crunch came one Sunday morning when we were leading worship from behind the large, polished, wooden podium. The auditorium was thickly carpeted complete with heavy gold drapes and pews that were firmly bolted to the floor.

As always, the team had prepared the room by coming an hour early to pray and worship around the room, to invite the presence of the Holy Spirit in the service to follow. Unfortunately, even with this preparation, once the congregation was there we often struggled. I think the struggle was both with the religious spirit that loves to inhabit religious environments, (especially on Sunday mornings) and also the acoustics in the room which led me to firmly believe that the devil is an architect! Each musical note was literally swallowed by the carpet, drapes and acoustic tiles on the ceiling.

That morning I began to lead a song of joyful praise and many of the people joined in clapping along with the rhythm. This wasn't unusual but the next thing was. "Step out from behind the podium and dance," said a clear unmistakable voice in my spirit.

"What?!" I reasoned.

"Don't just sing about it, do it," said the voice that I recognized as the Holy Spirit. I looked at the people, dressed in their Sunday best. "Dance before Me in front of them."

So, remembering the word about little children and feeling as foolish as a frog on a freeway, I stepped from behind the security of that podium and danced up and down across the front of the room. My joy was real and my heart sincere as I praised God with all my might.

Something broke in me that day. As I danced and others joined me, I realized that so often we talk and sing about what we are going to do in our praises yet we need to "just do it." I also saw something of the truth of what the Levites said to a people weary with sin and deprivation so many years before. "The joy of the Lord is your strength" (Nehemiah 8:10).

Have you ever seen a child stand still while expressing true joy? Neither have I.

Morris Chapman

Morris Chapman has spent more than 20 years in full-time ministry, teaching and leading praise and worship nationally and internationally. His primary focus is to lead believers into a deeper and more intimate relationship with the Lord through worship. He has recorded on both the Word/Nelson and Maranatha! Music labels. Morris is perhaps most well known for the many songs he has written including "Be Bold, Be Strong," "Bethlehem Morning" and "We Give You Praise."

The second of 12 children, Morris gave his life to the Lord at a very early age. Although he had never had any formal training, Morris began playing piano at age 11. He is currently one of the praise and worship leaders in the Maranatha Promise Band, ministering to thousands of men annually at Promise Keepers conferences around the nation.

Morris and his wife, Shirley, reside in Las Vegas, Nevada, along with their five children and three grandchildren.

Don't Quit—Submit

Most people think of me as a fluent writer and a good poet. However, they don't know English was one of my poorest subjects in school. I never enjoyed reciting poetry in front of the class and I dropped out of school in the tenth grade. Beyond this, I've never had any vocal, musical or writing training. (Don't let that stop you from learning to read or write and play by music. I'd also encourage you to learn to play by ear even if you can read music.) I believe that's the reason I lean more to a spontaneous style of worship.

Coming from a predominantly black gospel background, some close to me could not understand the transformation from soul gospel to a more contemporary style of ministry. Andre Crouch's "Live at Carnegie Hall" and his music had a large influence on me, but my deepest inspiration and encouragement comes from my wife of more than thirty years. My dear Shirley is the reason most of our songs got finished. Her "don't quit and don't give up" attitude has blessed many. I would have given up on many songs had it not been for her. As a matter of fact, there's a story behind every song we've received.

"Be Bold, Be Strong" came at a time when I was about to give up. I recall complaining about the size of some of my offerings and Mrs. Chapman showing me one of the old check stubs from the time I was employed as a janitor. She asked me whose payroll I would rather be on, or to paraphrase it, "Would you like to go back to Egypt?" (Smile)

"We Give You Praise" received such a cool reception when I first sang it I almost tossed it into the trash. Again it was my lovely wife's encouragement not to be swayed by that particular audience's response. "Broken Things" and "Lately" are other songs that received a similar response.

"In Remembrance Of You" is one of those rare spontaneous songs that comes all at once. It happened during communion in December of 1978. The same weekend I committed to full-time ministry.

"Bethlehem Morning" was more like a Cecil B. Demille epic, over two years in the making with countless changes. Let me explain the reason it took so long.

The real hold up was that I forgot that God creates these precious gifts, and I tried to write "Bethlehem Morning" on my own. I came up with some of the corniest lines you've ever heard. The second line of the first verse I knew would end with the word *still*. I kept trying to insert something about the shepherds in the field, *still*. Perhaps the Lord was saying, "Just be *still*, wait on Me as always."

One night my pastor at the time dropped by and asked if I was still struggling with the song. "What is your Scripture basis for this song?" he asked. "Isaiah 9," I answered. After he left I knelt down by the piano and confessed to the Lord that this song was His song, not mine, and that I was guilty of watching the charts instead of reaching hearts. Yes, that was the problem.

While still on my knees I was prompted to reach over and pick up a small King James Version Bible and read Isaiah 9. To my amazement the line of the second verse was repeated three times in that chapter. "His hand is stretched out still." As soon as we inserted the line in the song it was just a matter of minutes before the lyrics were complete. All that was left was to refine the melody and get the song into the hands of an arranger.

I believe that taught me to yield all to Him, especially my attitude. I still need to let Him have complete control at all times and with everything. I believe I am to seek Him for each line to make sure the words fit. More importantly, I am to commit my life to Him and line it up with His Word. I need to make sure I live *morally*, keep pure motives, and let Him fulfill His purpose. Then my *mission* will be complete.

> P.S. God is more impressed with *character* than *credentials*.

David Ruis

David Ruis has been involved in music and pastoral ministry over the last 14 years. He planted the Vineyard in Kelowna, British Columbia, Canada, with Wes Campbell in 1986. David co-pastored there until 1991 when the Lord led him and his family to Kansas City where he was an associate pastor and worship leader at Metro Vineyard. Currently David is preparing to plant a Vineyard in Winnipeg, Manitoba, Canada.

David has travelled extensively leading worship and teaching internationally. His heart is to see the Church rise up in passion for the Son, releasing godly character and radical obedience. The prophetic, renewal and mercy are themes that weave through his songs and teaching. David has led worship on two of Vineyard's "Touching the Father's Heart" recordings. Several of the songs he has penned are being used worldwide by the Church.

David and his wife, Anita, have four children. They reside in Kelowna and are on their way to Winnipeg.

Heart Unity

In my early days of leading worship I had the opportunity to lead worship for a major event outside my home church. The worship team I would be working with was a combination of people from various churches. They didn't know me at all and hardly knew each other. Circumstances dictated that we would have only one rehearsal the evening before the main event. I didn't know what songs were common to us, the skill level of the musicians I'd be playing with, etc. I was a little rattled.

As people began to show up for rehearsal, I had us form a circle first instead of going straight to our instruments to play music. Even though the pressure to get a list and start rehearsing was great, I felt we needed to connect at a heart level first, instead of just on a musical plane.

Before I knew it personal ministry was happening, the Kleenex was flying and we ended up around the piano worshipping together. Some hours later we were "listless" and hadn't rehearsed one song. But we had touched each other's lives and "knew" each other in the Lord's presence. We'd connected at a heart level.

The next night was glorious. The band trusted me, I trusted them. We just continued in our worship experience together. We were from different backgrounds, musical tastes and expressions yet we were united in worship.

From that point on whether I'm leading in a "foreign" context or building a new worship team, I look for the heart connection. Our unity must be found in something deeper than the music, the list, or the instruments.

Worshipping From Where We Are

Often we feel like Clark Kent needing to become Superman to get the job done. We have trouble being who we are, and worshipping from where we are. One evening my electric guitar player was late and the worship session was nearing. This was unusual for him and I wondered what was up.

Finally, he came struggling in. I realized something was wrong. He had his gear and began setting up, but as he was getting ready he told me he didn't feel like playing. Some hours before, he'd received word that a close friend had been killed in an accident. He was confused, angry and just not "into it."

I appreciated where he was coming from but expressed my desire for him to play. I didn't want to put any pressure on him and said that if he was grieving too much to play that was okay. But, if he felt like he couldn't worship until he felt better, that was not a good enough reason to not worship.

I asked him to just play from where he was at. I told him to lift his pain and confusion to the Lord *in* worship. Let the guitar speak his cry to the Lord. He didn't have to feel better to play, just play how he *felt*.

The guitar that night reflected passion like I've never heard. The solos were not just neat riffs; they spoke and people were touched. I was lifted to the Lord in a way I rarely touch in the corporate environment.

We in North America and the western world need to touch this dynamic. The Psalms are a constant reflection of worshiping from "where you are."

Don't Forget the People

As I've reflected on worship leading I've often pondered the responsibility of "taking" people somewhere in worship. I was often told, "You're there for God. Don't worry about the people or anything else. Just worship!"

So I would press in and often found myself becoming angry at the congregation. They weren't entering in, or they did not seem to understand.

One morning as I was leading it was as though the Lord said, "What are you doing here? You don't need to be doing this in front of all these people!"

I began to realize that although my focus is on God, I was there to serve the people. I was to touch them where they're at and draw them into worship. I could worship at home. I didn't need to do it in front of a crowd.

I know that as I worship it inspires the people, but if I go so far ahead and leave everyone behind, I haven't reached my goal. It is like having one eye on God, and one eye on the people. I began to get in touch with the hurts and needs of the people. I learned to "feel the pulse" of the congregation and lead as a servant understanding where they were.

Worshipping God is important when leading but please don't forget about the people.

Eddie Espinosa

Eddie Espinosa was born in Los Angeles, California, and was raised in the Catholic church where he served as an altar boy. In 1969, at the age of 15, Eddie gave his heart to Jesus Christ in a deeper way. On the following day he was taken to a youth rally where he saw Andrae Crouch leading people into the presence of God. Eddie immediately knew he was called to do the same.

Although he is a pastor, Eddie is most widely known as a worship leader and songwriter. He has composed such popular songs as "You Are The Mighty King," "Most Of All" and "Change My Heart, Oh God." His heart's desire is to see Psalm 67 come to pass: "May the peoples praise You, oh God, may all the peoples praise You."

Eddie's passion for the Lord is evident in his music and worship leading. He has been a worship leader at the Vineyard in Anaheim for over 12 years.

Eddie and his wife, Elsie, have two children and reside in Anaheim, California.

To Make a List or Not Make a List? That Is the Question!

One day one of the members on the worship team said to me that he thought that the worship was flat and dull because I was using a prepared list of songs. Because I respect the people who are a part of our music ministry I took his comment very seriously. I even prayed about it. "O God, if the way I'm planning or even the fact that I am planning is getting in the way of what You want to do in our worship, I ask You to correct me, to teach me, even to rebuke me if necessary." I continued on and told the Lord that I did not want to be a hindrance to what He was wanting to do.

At the end of my prayer time I made a deal with the Lord. I said, "Lord, I would like to do a little experiment. I'm going to pray and prepare just like I normally do when I lead worship. I'm even going to make a list, just like usual. But I'm not going to give that list to the worship team. And, one more thing, Lord, I'd like permission, just this once, to disobey You." What I meant by that last statement was that if, during the worship set, I felt led to deviate from my prepared list and do a different song spontaneously, I would continue to go by the list. As I prayed I felt like this was all acceptable to the Lord.

On the given Sunday morning, the worship team prayed and went over a few songs, but I didn't let anybody see my list. I kept it hidden. Nobody knew I even had a list. As I was leading worship I kept going down the list that I had made, exactly as I had written it.

Worship went really well. It went so well, in fact, that the same team member who had confronted me came up to me after worship and said, "Oh Eddie, worship was fantastic! It was so great; I just can't believe it was so good!" he said. "I betcha I know why, too. It's 'cause you got rid of the stinkin' list."

"Well," I responded, "actually I took what you said very seriously." Then I told him the whole process that I had gone through. I finished by explaining, "As a matter of fact I did go by the list and I did the songs in the exact same order." The look on his face was great. I wish I had had a camera.

As a worship leader I always try to find the best way to lead worship. One of the things that I have found to be important is to seek the Lord beforehand and to prepare myself by making a song list. I see leading worship very much like preparing a sermon. A good pastor prepares carefully ahead of time, putting much time and prayer into a sermon. Without this preparation he is, in essence, saying that he is unwilling to put the necessary time into prayer, meditation and listening to the Lord.

Jesus said that He only did what He saw the Father doing. Moses followed the pillar of cloud and the pillar of fire and only moved when they moved. In the same way we as worship leaders need to be followers of the Holy Spirit. He is really the worship leader. We are simply following what He wants to emphasize when we lead.

The issue is not whether or not to make a list. The issue is that if you make a list, make it according to what you believe the Holy Spirit is telling you for that particular service. I believe we need to prepare and plan, yet be flexible and leave room for the nudging of the Holy Spirit during the service to lead us in another direction.

What I do is to pray during the week and ask the Lord to bring songs to my mind. Then I write them down. I also ask the person that will be giving the message what topic and/or particular Scripture he will be speaking on. Often times the Lord will give me songs that go along with the topic without even knowing what that topic is. I believe we need to be flexible and plan according to what the Lord is saying.

The "G" Factor

There was a pastors conference going on and I was leading worship. About 2,000 pastors and leaders were in attendance. Halfway through the worship set the Lord told me to "go into repentance songs."

I remember arguing with the Lord and saying, "Lord, this is a pastor's conference and all these guys are leaders and pastors. They're right on with You." Then, very distinctly, He once again said, "Repentance songs." I finally conceded to what I was certain God was saying. I began to sing Psalm 51, "Create in Me a Clean Heart," "Change My Heart, Oh God," "It's Your Blood That Cleanses Me," and another series of songs about repentance and forgiveness and the blood of Christ.

After that we went into some more songs talking about intimacy with God, drawing close to Him, and the Father loving us. I assumed that there would be a word of prophecy or encouragement given that had to do with repentance. Nothing happened! I thought, "Well maybe the message is on repentance and our need to be before

God." Still nothing happened. Then I thought maybe somebody was going to sing a special number. Still nothing. By this time I was feeling very defeated, certain that I had completely missed God.

Finally about 45 minutes after I had finished leading worship, the pastor that was in charge of the meeting looked at the congregation and said, "I really feel that someone here has a word from the Lord for us." A brother in the back row raised his hand and stood up and said, "I feel that there are people here who have seen their ministry and are performing their ministry as though they are hirelings and not as shepherds." That simple statement broke the hearts of a lot of pastors and leaders. As a result about 300 pastors and leaders came up to the altar, weeping and repenting. It was a wonderful time where God was meeting people's needs.

To me the question was, "Did I cause that to happen as a worship leader?" No! I believe that there are two things a worship leader cannot take for himself and they both begin with the letter "G." The first is "glory" when things go well and the second is "guilt" when things don't go quite as planned. I did not cause the time of ministry to happen. God was going to do what He wanted to do with or without me. But it was such a blessing for me to take part in what God was doing. It was a perfect example for me of doing what the Father wants instead of what my own rational judgment thought was appropriate at the time. In following the direction of the Lord, we need obedience and flexibility.

Eugene Greco

Eugene Greco was the worship leader for Integrity's Hosanna! Music's "Exalt the Lord." The former music director at Christ for the Nations Institute of Biblical Studies in Stony Brook, New York, he now travels from place to place ministering a fresh word from God through music, teaching and preaching.

Eugene is perhaps best known for his songs. He has composed congregational favorites such as, "Mighty Is Our God," "God Is the Strength of My Heart," and "Purify My Heart."

Together with his wife, Joy, Eugene has founded His Banner Ministries, *based in northern New Jersey where they live. He and Joy and their two children often travel and minister together as a family. Together they have a heart for the nations and a desire to see people of all backgrounds come into the presence of the Lord.*

Hosting Hungry Worshippers

Sometimes the voice of need speaks louder than the voice of God.

When I was a new believer, I was invited to be a worship leader at the local church I was attending. I would have liked to think it was due to my great spiritual maturity. However, looking back I now realize it probably had more to do with the fact that I could play the piano and sing at the same time!

Things were drastically different looking out over the congregation from the front of the church. What was my job description again? Oh, yeah... I was to lead them into the presence of God. I soon discovered the fact that this place (the presence of the Lord) did not interest a great many of the people out there. I would have never known it, because they were always behind me—until now! My perspective had totally changed!

So, how did I get them moving in the general direction of God? My natural reasoning suggested to get behind them and start whipping. I treated God's people as cattle instead of sheep. After all, I did live in dairy country. In our county, there were more cows than sheep.

I quickly grew very frustrated as I realized that the more I tried, the more they scattered. The more they scattered, the harder my job became. I wearied myself trying to make something happen.

My pastor was a calm man. The only advice he had to give me in worship leading was perhaps the most important thing anyone ever shared with me on the subject. All he said was, "The best way to get someone hungry is to eat in front of them."

I have heard it said that half of worship leading is being a worshipper, and the other half is leading. (Sounds simple, doesn't it?!) I had to face the challenge that I could not lead anyone to a place that I had not been myself (many times over). I needed to be a worshipper when no one else was around (except God, of course).

I learned that people did not respond well to a leader that expected something of them that he didn't do himself. (Oh, how the truth hurts before it heals!) Sheep seem to have an innate sense about these things. They don't do what you say, but rather, what you do. I learned to be genuine as I stood on the platform before them.

I constantly put myself through a reality check making sure that what I was before the people was the same as what I was when I was alone with God. If we need some objective input to help us undergo a reality check, (and our spouse is unavailable—smile) we can simply ask the junior high kids what they perceive. They can quickly spot a phony.

There were times I had to go ahead and meet with God even though no one seemed to join me. I have to admit there were times I didn't mind. The pendulum so easily swings to the other extreme. I realized I could quickly forget about the people and just get lost in God. But, then I read my job description: *Worship Leader.* The evidence of being a good leader is to have a follower. I needed a heart for God and a heart for His people. I began to pray for the heart of David. He was able to soar in the heavenlies but he also shepherded God's people with integrity of heart (see Psalm 78:72). It can't be one or the other—it has to be both.

I finally resigned to the fact that what I desired to see would not happen overnight (sorry to disappoint those who are still looking for the push-button method!). I needed to develop a team of people who could lead by their example.

As a team, we would learn to come into services ready to minister—to give rather than receive. If we were regularly meeting with God, we wouldn't need the service time to get our "fix." Instead, we would learn to be sensitive to the Lord *and* to the people. We learned not to focus too much on where the people were—just enough to be aware of their needs. God was and always is to be the focal point. If need be, we would turn our backs on the people from time to time (figuratively speaking, like a shepherd would when leading the sheep) and give a call, saying: "This is where we are going. The water's fine."

One day I discovered a lot of the frustrations I once knew no longer existed. To this day there is no greater joy than being together with God's people as one body in the presence of the Lord. There the Lord commands His blessing and reveals His life.

Worship and Evangelism: The Powerful Connection

A few years ago, my wife had the opportunity to visit her native Sweden and attend a conference. She was drawn to one workshop dealing with the ministry of music in the church. The leader of this session made a statement something like this: "Of course, everyone knows that *worship* and *evangelism* have nothing to do with each other."

There was a day when we might have thought that way. However, over the years our experience has taught us differently. One such experience happened early on in the ministry while I was the worship leader and college pastor at a local church in upstate New York.

My wife and I were invited to join a team for an evangelistic thrust at the University of Vermont, a college campus that seemed to have a long-standing resistance to the gospel. It was a great opportunity to lend support to a struggling Christian fellowship group that met on campus. Those days proved to be days when God would do a new thing in our hearts.

The strategy was for us to "blitz" certain parts of the campus with one-on-one evangelism and open-air preaching. (This was the first time I ever attempted such a daring feat!) We went to a certain busy thoroughfare and one of us stood on a bench to preach while the others mingled and attempted to get into conversations with those passing by. I can still remember how dry and hard the spiritual ground was! We did our best to be faithful to our cause. Finally, after a series of fruitless attempts, one of the team members suggested we just begin to praise God. My wife had her flute, someone a guitar, and someone else a tambourine. So, we went to it! It was a totally new and different concept. (This was years before hearing about "praise marches" and seeing the rising popularity of such events.)

We soon discovered God meant what He said when we saw His presence fill that place as He was "enthroned upon our praises" (see Psalm 22:3). The spiritual impact of our preaching changed as we flowed with greater inspiration and anointing. Also, we began to see more of an openness in our personal contacts. I recall finishing one conversation and looking around seeing the other team members actively involved in their conversations. I went over and sat on a bench, picked up the guitar and began to sing. I was not singing for anyone there. I was simply lifting my song to God. Out of the corner of my eye I noticed a young man ride his bike right over next to me. He stood motionless. When I finished the song, he told me how he was riding down the street feeling very depressed and heard me singing and it made him "feel better." I invited him to the meeting we were having that evening. I was amazed at the ease I had in sharing with him that day.

A little while later we all took a lunch break and found the nearest cafeteria. When we entered the dining room I noticed a piano in the corner. I immediately felt a tug at my heart and knew I was to ask permission to play it. God gave me favor with the manager and I must have sat at that piano for two hours! I exhausted my repertoire playing and singing every song I knew. It was interesting to see the effect. There were some who got up and left, but then there were others who were thirsting and hungering for more than lunch. A couple of our guys led a young man to the Lord while the band (the one-man-band, that is) played on. This convert later became a key leader of the campus Christian fellowship!

I came to learn a most powerful truth that day which affects my whole life and ministry: *When I touch the heart of God, God touches the hearts of men.*

Even the recording of the Hosanna worship tape, "Exalt the Lord," proved to be a highly evangelistic event. I never gave an "altar call" yet we have heard of person after person giving their hearts to the Lord that night as we worshipped God! One of the converts was a visiting scholar from Tibet who spoke no English! He told a Chinese friend who had invited him that he wanted to "know" the God that these people worshipped!

These are just a couple of examples. I could go on and on. God has placed this truth deep within our hearts. "*Judah* (literally "praise") *must plow*" if we want to see a harvest (see Hosea 10:11).

Vivien Hibbert

Vivien Hibbert was born in New Zealand. She began full-time ministry in 1977 with her husband, Michael, as a teacher of praise and worship. Michael and Vivien have produced three music tapes and written a manual on praise and worship entitled Music Ministry, *which is used in their praise and worship seminars.*

They ministered as singers and teachers of praise and worship in several countries before joining the staff of a church in Reno, Nevada, in 1985. Michael and Vivien moved to Texas in 1990 as the ministers of worship and fine arts at Shady Grove Church in Dallas. Vivien continues to travel from time to time, ministering in churches and conferences internationally and throughout the U.S.

Michael and Vivien reside with their son in the Dallas area.

My Coal for His Diamonds

I am a great believer in the practice of praying honest and dangerous prayers—prayers that impact the heart and soul of our lives and ministry. I like prayers such as Moses prayed: "Lord, show me your glory!" Or prayers we might pray like, "Do whatever you need to do in my life that I might be all that you need me to be," or "Soften my heart, Lord"... very dangerous prayers! As a worship leader, I sense the continuous call to personal growth and change into the likeness of Jesus. My desire to lead worship has been born out of these prayers and a desire to see and know the presence of God individually and corporately amongst His people.

An example of one of these life-changing prayers occurred on one of our routine travel-home-after-several-weeks-of-tiring-ministry days in the heat of a blistering summer.

On the previous day, I had lost a significant diamond out of a precious family ring. I made a bargain with the Lord that I would not cry over this diamond (no matter how valuable, no matter how irreplaceable, no matter how meaningful) so long as He would create a "diamond" within my heart. This was a very dangerous prayer as diamonds are made from the long-term pressure that is placed upon coal. My prayer opened up a chain of events over the next few days that would provoke some serious diamond mining in my heart.

As my family and I entered a small town in California, our car broke down (again). We were only passing through on a fifteen hundred mile journey, but now things looked serious. "Praise God!" I said. "We are right outside the City Mission. Some obliging Christian will help us move the car to the side of the road." I knocked on the door and after a few minutes, it cracked open about two inches. A nervous head appeared through the crack. Help was not forthcoming. With a flourish of an "I'm-sorry-but-we-cannot-help" attitude, we were dismissed to solve our own problem. It also happened to be Memorial Day, and the only garage open was two miles out of town through the hot desert.

After a towing fee (increased, of course, because of the public holiday) and several hours of investigatory labor, the mechanic presented us with another, "I'm sorry" story. We had to stay overnight and purchase the part that was needed from the auto parts store. Unfortunately, the auto parts store did not carry this particular part. "I'm sorry," they said, "you will have to stay another night as we need to order this part from the closest city."

Various problems with the acquisition of food and lodging caused further pitiful, "I'm sorrys." We began to suspect a small-town plot to take advantage of unsuspecting travelers.

Late the following afternoon, once the part had arrived and the mechanic had spent several more hours on installation, we were greeted with yet another, "I'm sorry, you will have to stay another night!" The auto parts store had ordered the wrong part! With great aplomb, I picked up the part, tucked it under my arm and walked purposefully through the long, hot desert to the auto parts store. "May I please speak to the manager?" I asked politely yet thoroughly exasperated. "I'm sorry," replied the person behind the counter, "the manager is not available."

It was at this moment that things snapped inside. I am not sure if the Lord was doing some serious poking at the huge coal deposits in my heart or if there were some other lessons to be learned during this moment of crisis. With one movement, I gathered all the things that were on display on the counter and threw them into the air. My actions summoned the immediate presence of the manager and the entire police force of this small town—two squad cars with lights ablaze and sirens blaring. One police officer entered the store, and without the courtesy of our now customary, "I'm sorry," heaved me over the counter and twisted my arms up my back to the point of serious pain. I was then handcuffed and thrown into the back of his stifling hot squad car for a long time of "cooling off" (his car was sealed for officer protection).

At this point, any truly spiritual worship leader would testify to the salvation of the police officer, the parts store manager, the mechanic and half of the town. I, on the other hand, can only testify to the shame I felt as God revealed a serious coal deposit of anger, pride and self-pity in my heart.

The adjustment to the car was completed after one more night, but the corrections continue within my heart. The depth and resistance of the coal deposits never cease to amaze me, but I am determined to continue the process of holy exchange: My coal for His diamonds!

Mark Altrogge

Mark Altrogge is a songwriter with a different flair. His particular interest and burden is to write songs of worship with doctrinal content in a style that is relevant and exciting to this generation. His songs include "Forever Grateful," "I Stand in Awe," "Oh Most High," and "I Have a Destiny." His songs have been recorded on Integrity's Hosanna! Music and Word Records' HeartCry label, as well as by such folks as Annie Herring and Glad.

Mark considers himself the most blessed man on earth. He's crazy about his four kids and his wife, Kristi, who laughs at most of his jokes. He gets to pastor and preach at Lord of Life Church, a great bunch of folks in Indiana, Pennsylvania. A former rock musician, he loves electric guitar in worship and anywhere else. He likes to read Puritan devotional books and mystery novels. He is a seriously frustrated fisherman, though he doesn't know enough to quit. In addition, he's constantly amazed by the mercy and grace of God.

The Man Who Would Not Dance

One of the most liberating experiences for me was learning though the ministries of C. J. Mahaney and Terry Virgo about the concept of motivating by grace. But first let me give you an experience of motivation by pressure. This occurred years ago, when I was young, zealous, legalistic and fairly stupid at times (I'm no longer young, hopefully not legalistic, hopefully still zealous and working on the last one).

A friend of mine, whom I shall call Bradley, was pastoring our church. One Sunday as I was leading worship, I called upon (maybe it was more like a command than a call) the church to dance. Bradley who shared my aforementioned qualities, looked around the church to make sure everyone was dancing. But in the back, like a lone tree in a field, stood Rick (name changed). Rick was the kind of guy you couldn't tell to do anything, especially dance. He stood there, arms crossed, staring straight ahead. Bradley could not believe his eyes. So there in the midst of a rousing celebration before the Lord, the showdown occurred. Bradley pointed to Rick and mouthed, "You, dance!" Rick just stared back like Clint Eastwood as if to say, "Make me." Needless to say, Bradley lost that battle. Rick, the lone tree, stood there for the rest of the song, arms crossed, staring straight ahead, not so much as tapping his toe.

In those days, worship leading to me was a "me-against-them" affair. I assumed that these people didn't want to worship, that they were all apathetic and complacent and that it was my job to somehow whip them into praising God. And so, week after week I'd exhort with phrases like, "Let's worship like we really mean it," knowing that, of course, these lazy slugs didn't mean it. I was the only one left who really loved God and really loved to worship—except for Bradley, that is. We were the remnant of true worshipers in the earth.

But later on I learned a wonderful lesson: When someone receives Jesus Christ, he receives a new heart; then the Holy Spirit moves and motivates him to love Jesus. I learned that believers really do want to worship; they really do love God. God is changing them and transforming them and conforming them to His Son. Sometimes, after a week in the world, they may need a little help to get rolling, but it's not because they don't love God or want to praise Him. I found out that grace means, "This I know: God is for me." God is for the people. He loves them. Can't wait to pour out His Spirit on them. Can't wait to help them.

Now if God is so much for these people, shouldn't the worship leader be also? Looking at the people in this new way transformed my worship leading style. Now when I encourage or exhort I attempt to remind them of Who God is and all He's done for them. God is for them, and He's a great and wonderful God. I found that when I quit pressuring them I was somehow released from pressure myself. Worship leading became fun and the joy that God intends it to be.

By the way, Bradley's been set free too.

David Wright

David Wright serves as minister of music at The Living Word in Middletown, Ohio. Previously he worked with Kenneth Copeland Ministries overseeing the recording and production of music-related products while serving as worship leader for The Church at Eagle Mountain. For two years David worked with Willie George Ministries scoring the music for the nationally syndicated children's TV show, "The Gospel Bill Show." In addition to these positions he has written, arranged and produced for artists such as Kenneth Copeland, Len Mink, Kim Clement and John Stevenson.

David and his wife, Adrienne, travel to churches and conferences, teaching principles of praise and worship. David and Adrienne reside in Middletown, Ohio, with their two children.

People or Possessions?

Over the years I've found that one of the hardest positions to fill on a worship team is that of the keyboardist. Finding someone who meets all the criteria is like manna from heaven. Can they play by ear? Can they play by music? Can they play in whatever key is necessary? The list goes on and on. As any worship leader will tell you, a competent keyboardist is truly a treasured blessing.

During my first official assignment as a worship leader I was privileged to work with such a person. God had truly shone upon me after all those Sundays of playing for myself. This young man, who we will call Josh for the story's sake, had a heart for worship, could flow in the Spirit, and could decipher those strange chord charts I continually put in front of him. What a team we made.

Things were going along quite nicely. The church was growing. The worship team was growing. I was very comfortable with the status quo. That is, until the phone rang.

I was sitting at my desk being creative when an

acquaintance from a large national ministry called. They were in need of a keyboardist who could travel with their crusade team, one of those guys who fit all the above mentioned criteria. I told him I didn't know of anyone right off the top of my head but, if I thought of someone, he'd be the first to know.

As soon as I hung up the phone I heard "the *Voice*"! I couldn't believe it. Had God just said that Josh was the one anointed to go? Surely not! I had prayed and believed for this treasured possession. I couldn't imagine having to play for myself again. So, I told the Lord, "He's mine and that's the way it will stay!" The Lord had brought him to me; surely He wouldn't take him from me.

For the next week the Holy Spirit dealt with me night and day. When I woke up He was speaking, and when I went to sleep He was speaking. Was Josh a possession to bargain with or a person with a calling and destiny to fulfill? Finally I quit being stubborn and repented. Josh the child of God was more important than Josh the keyboardist.

The next day I called the music director for the large national ministry and told him all about Josh and where to get a hold of him. The day after that a very excited Josh called and told me all about a great job offer that he had been praying and believing for. Of course I said, "Go for it!"

I'm glad the Lord taught me early in my ministry that

those I work with are gifts to be treasured, not possessions to use and exploit. People have needs, callings, and dreams waiting to be fulfilled.

Josh has gone on to become a worship leader with a national youth ministry and I recently had the privilege to help him produce one of his first worship tapes. As for playing for myself, well, that has been a blessing that afforded me the opportunity to lead worship in a lot of places I would not have been able to otherwise.

How About Heart

For eight years I worked with some of the most talented musicians in the music business. My worship team was made up of professional musicians who did studio work and traveled extensively throughout America.

For that reason I had a lot of flexibility and latitude as to the music we used for our worship services. One blessing was to walk in with a chart that no one had seen or heard and perform it accurately and effectively. Not only were these guys great musicians, they were true worshippers also.

However, after eight years my wife and I went to a

small church that needed help establishing their music program. We had made a one-year commitment and were ready to get to work. Our first rehearsal was quite a surprise.

What we found was a group of singers who had never worked together in groups of any kind before. The drummer was not sure what two and four was, much less where it was. The bass player had never played bass before and the guitar player kept asking me how to make the chords. I kept thinking, "How are we ever going to get in the presence of God Sunday without having a major disaster?"

All the way home from practice I kept wondering what I had done wrong. Surely God was punishing me for something. I felt like I had been banished to the back side of the desert never to be heard from again. Little did I know that I would learn one of the most important lessons of my life with the little ragtag group.

After a few weeks of rehearsals and services I noticed something that proved to be a key. Though these guys lacked technical ability, they had more of a heart for God than most people I knew. Our rehearsals ended up being worship services themselves.

The team was becoming just that—a team. Laying aside their inhibitions, they were learning to pray together, worship together, flow in the Spirit together, and bear their hearts to God without worrying about what everyone else thought. Our church services became extensions of our rehearsals.

For the next year I emphasized worshipping God from our hearts. We pressed in to know the heart of God. While we worked to improve our technical skill, the team's ability to flow in the Spirit and lead that congregation into the throne room grew by leaps and bounds.

Fifteen months after arriving, three of the team had become worship leaders themselves and everyone had learned enough to find their way around a piece of music. As my wife and I left there for our next assignment we knew we were going to miss these guys a lot. We learned more about worshipping God from this group than all the seminars and books had taught us.

God took a spoiled worship leader used to the best technically and taught me what I knew in my head but had never experienced. God is still more interested in our heart for Him than in technical ability. While you may lack technical expertise, if your heart is truly after Him you can be light years ahead of everyone else spiritually. That is not an excuse to stop pursuing technical excellence, however. The thing to remember is that no matter what you accomplish technically, God is really after your heart.

Even today I am reminded each service of this fact. We have a lady in our church who lacks the technical expertise to play with the team for worship. However, I have never met anyone who could create an atmosphere for the anointing while playing the piano as she does. I have her play before every service.

I pray that as we strive to do our best, we remember that what God really wants is our hearts.

Bob
Mason

Bob Mason, associate pastor of the North Church in Carrollton, Texas, directs the music and arts ministries which consist of over 150 people. He also serves as the praise and worship leader and is the dean of the North Church School of Theology. Additionally, Bob assists Dr. Lawrence Kennedy, senior pastor of the North Church, in directing Church on the Rock International which oversees 1400 churches worldwide. He also travels and ministers in praise and worship seminars and leadership conferences.

Pastor Bob's ministry experience includes having served for seven years on staff at Christ for the Nations Institute in Dallas, Texas, where he was dean of music. There he travelled as director of the singing group, "Living Praise," and ministered in 30 nations on four continents. He received bachelor of music education from Henderson State University and is currently finishing a master's in music and divinity degree from Oral Roberts University.

Bob and his wife, Debbie, and their daughter reside in Carrollton, Texas.

The Mardi Gras Miracle

A few years ago, when I was at Mardi Gras, our music team, "Living Praise" ministered at Jackson Square. We diligently sought the Lord, fasting and praying for weeks. The brass section of our group was very good, and I thought that we should do all the songs with brass to attract the people. We had great crowds of people—literally two or three thousand—on the corner of Jackson Square listening to us. But the moment the songs were over, the people would scatter. We would start to share the gospel with them, and they were gone. I said, "God, we have to get through to these people. We are wasting our time here."

The Lord answered, "Just worship Me. Don't sing about Me, sing to Me."

To be honest, I felt a little bit foolish. I closed my eyes tightly so I could not see anyone. I lifted my hands and began to worship with all my might. We began singing warfare songs about leaping walls and tearing down strongholds. When I opened my eyes, I saw that people were stunned. They were hooked. They could not leave. They were wondering what in the world these guys were going to do next. We were just worshipping God. We started dancing around the stage, letting go of our control and letting the Holy Spirit take control. As we did that, many people started receiving the Lord. Approximately 1,850 people were born again in a five-day period as we ministered with others from Christ For The Nations.

A few weeks later, a dear pastor friend told me an incredible story. He had a man come into his church who was absolutely filled with demons. He went through a glorious deliverance. Several days later at a backyard picnic, some tapes were playing. The man perked up, went over, and asked who was singing. When told that it was "Living Praise," he answered, "They were at Mardi Gras, weren't they? I knew I recognized that spirit." He had been in the satanist church for ten years. He visited church services all around the country and sent "fiery darts" at the pastors. He would either plant lewd thoughts in their minds or cause confusion so that they became lost in their sermon.

He said that when he went to Mardi Gras with his coven, a demon stopped them as they started getting close to Jackson Square where our group was singing. It spoke very clearly and said, "Do not dare go near them. If you see one of them coming down the street, turn and run the other direction. Don't even get close to those people. Run as fast as you can. Don't have any contact with them, and don't get within earshot of their music."

This man had thought the devil was the ultimate power, but he realized there was something that the demons feared and that it paralyzed their power. When he went into a church in New Orleans and could not disrupt the pastor, he knew something had happened to him when he heard the praise and worship music. Consequently, he was saved and delivered. There is awesome power in our worship.

Praise and worship effects all areas of our lives. Our church members and the world need to see the validity of worship. They must realize that we are not simply singing songs but releasing the habitation of God in our very being. Their attitude and their actions are positive reinforcements through that praise and worship. This releases healing in their spirits, minds and physical bodies. If people come into a service and are really led into worship, it will strengthen them in every way. The authority and power of God will be established in their hearts as the praise is joined with the Word.

"Let the high praises of God be in their mouth, and a two-edged sword in their hand, to execute vengeance on the nations, and punishments on the peoples; to bind their kings with chains, and their nobles with fetters of iron; to execute on them the written judgment–this honor have all His saints. Praise the Lord!" (Psalm 149:6-9).

Ray Hughes

Ray Hughes is an inspiring speaker and humorist. He is founder and president of the Worship Congress based in Nashville, Tennessee, and the visionary for America Arise. Ray has made several appearances on national network television. He has also conducted numerous praise and worship conferences and evangelistic crusades in Russia. Ray has served local churches as worship leader, associate pastor and senior pastor. He is active in the music business as a music publisher and record producer.

Ray brings the best out of a variety of instruments, and his singing and songwriting is extraordinary and poignant. Ray's musical past has brought him from the blue- grass hills of Kentucky as a child picking on the front porch between grandpa's stories to one of the most prolific songwrit- ers and versatile musicians today.

His dream is to see the King of Kings high and lifted up, inhabiting the worship of a people of truth that are sub- mitted to and dominated by the Spirit of the living God.

Ray and his wife, Denise, along with their three chil-dren live in Lebanon, Tennessee.

Where Are My Steel Guitar Players?

Some years ago I was called upon by a pastor to come and minister at his church. I was scheduled to fly to his city on Sunday afternoon, minister at the evening service and a special Monday evening service and fly back out on Tuesday. When he picked me up at the airport I remembered him from a conference I had spoken at earlier in the year.

As we drove from the airport we briefly discussed the wonderful move of God we had experienced at that conference, and he voiced a genuine desire to see a release of God in his church. He felt that my being there was timely and that God was doing great things with his musicians. Then he made a request. "In tonight's service our praise team will be ministering and I would like you to make mental notes of areas in our music and worship that need attention. The service tomorrow evening will be just for our musicians. I would like you to share the things you think we can improve on and minister in whatever way you consider appropriate." He then dropped me off at my hotel and said he would be back to pick me up in about an hour.

We arrived at the church about ten minutes before the service was to begin. The parking lot was full and people were filing into the church. The musicians were tuning up and the sounds of pre-service fellowship were rolling down the hall into the pastor's office where we were chatting. He quickly glanced at his watch, grabbed my hand and prayed a thirty-second prayer for eternal anointing. We were out the door, down the hall and into the auditorium through a side door before I could pop a breath mint.

It was there that I was suddenly blasted into the awareness that "The Band" had started.

Let me introduce you to "The Band":

- Beverly Baptist on the piano was rocking and swatting the keys open-handedly as if she was trying to kill a mouse scurrying on the keyboard.
- Myrna Methodist on the organ, sat perched with her head bowed, one eye closed, bare left foot waving and bouncing consistently a half-beat behind, left hand sustaining at least an octave of notes moaning a minor chord against a major right hand and pulling stops as if to land a Cessna in a corn field.
- Thurman the Thumper on booming bass, muting

and popping most notes except for the ones that were accidently sustained only to cause a tingling effect to the hair on my legs.

- The Marvelous Mario Metronome on the triple-bass electronic drums, who was obviously a Grand Funk Railroad fan in an earlier life.
- Tommy Twelve-String, Bubba Bluegrass, Jimmy Jerk-A-Lot and Hot Lick Herbert on guitars—their combined sound brought to mind Willie Nelson and Eddie Van Halen playing dueling guitars to Lester Flatt and Earl Scrugg's "Foggy Mountain Breakdown."
- And last, but not least, was little Tammy No Tune on the piercing piccolo.

Then, of course, there were the vocalists:

The Holy-Spirit-Led (which way did He go?!) World Reaction Singers graciously led by worship leader (If-I-close-my-eyes-they'll-never-see-me) Sammy Sedate (who happens to be a Leon Spinks look-alike).

And holding it all together from the first row was Sister Ethel and her Tasmanian tambourine, formerly with the Bun-on-the-Head Bunch from Days-Gone-By, Arkansas. (The names have all been changed to protect the guilty.)

As I stood there evaluating the situation and trying to maintain some clarity of thought, I just raised my hands, closed my eyes and thanked God they didn't have a steel guitar player.

In the midst of the pandemonium and chaos of flying notes and feedback, God began speaking to me and I began to understand some things. For one, as I stood there it very gradually became obvious to me, "Ah, Majesty. Majesty. Yes, that's it, Majesty. The song they're doing is `Majesty'!"

Secondly, I realized that without a proper understanding of our roles in His presence, musicians sometimes take the position of whoever gets there first wins.

Thirdly, God answered a question that had been in my heart for years, "Where did the word `Charismaniacs' come from?!"

I know you would undoubtedly like to hear some of the pearls of great wisdom I brought forth to the musicians on Monday night as well as the godly counsel I gave to the pastor. However, to be quite honest, I can't tell you the rest of the story: it's too depressing.

He that hath an undamaged ear, let him hear.

I'm sure that there has been a time in all our lives when we asked the question, "Is God looking at this situation and laughing? Or is He crying?" I believe that in this particular situation He was laughing. He heard all the bad notes and the many rhythmical and metrical inconsistencies. He saw all the facial contortions and religious gestures being performed in the name of worship. And as ridiculous as it may sound, I believe His laughter could be heard throughout heaven.

Understand that I know God desires excellence and

that skill is very important. I realize there is no excuse for musical ignorance or laziness. However, when we take the music of all the different lifestyles, denominational backgrounds, musical preferences, nationalities and cultural as well as educational influences that determine who we are musically and put them all together into one 45-minute explosion on Sunday, I believe that what He sees the most are the pure hearts that have been cleansed by the blood of His Son. I think He looks around, laughs, and says, "Hey! Where are my steel guitar players?!"

Chris Bowater

For more than 20 years Chris Bowater has been at the heart of the worship revolution that has taken place in the church in the United Kingdom and others countries. With 10 major albums, two books and hundreds of songs to his credit, Chris has traveled extensively as an artist, worship leader and speaker. Working from his home in Lincoln, UK, and the large and growing New Life Christian Centre, Chris has visited all parts of the British Isles and numerous other countries. His songs are sung in scores of languages around the world.

Chris is constantly seeking to explore the cutting edge of music. His albums reflect strong classical and jazz influences. He graduated from the Royal College of Music, London, with a specific interest in composition and conducting. Becoming a school teacher, Chris developed communication skills and the ability to integrate contemporary and traditional music styles. Chris seeks to be a facilitator through his training programs, a bridge-builder (bringing churches together) through his conferences and an inspiration through his concerts and worship celebrations.

Chris and his wife, Lesley, have five children.

Hearing God's Voice

What does the *voice* of God sound like to you? Do you know when He is speaking to you? When our triplets, Mark, Hannah, and Sara were babies, friends who visited our home were astonished that we were capable of distinguishing one child's crying voice from the others'. I do realize that yelling infants tend to sound the same, unless of course you live with them. One soon learns to discern the little characteristic squeaks and gurgles. Recognition comes out of relationship. Worship must emanate from a real relationship with God our Father—a relationship of talking *and* listening.

Some years ago, I heard of a pastor who would personally interview people in his congregation entering into membership in his church. He had standard questions that he would ask, including, "What does the voice of God sound like to you?" His own teenage son was a candidate for membership. The pastor kept to his normal format.

"What does the voice of God sound like to you, son?" he inquired. Without so much as a moment's hesitation he replied, "Dad, He sounds just like you." That's such a good answer. The voice of his heavenly Father was as real and as clear as his own Dad's. That young man had a real relationship with God. I long for my children to hear God in the same way. It will be even better if they respond to His voice a little more readily than they do sometimes to mine!

"To hear God speak" has such grand and spiritual overtones. One at least expects an audible voice, perhaps a vision or two, maybe fire or a mighty rushing wind. How dramatic... how reassuringly real. Imagine musing horizontally in the doze zone on a lazy summer afternoon, only to hear the unmistakable voice of God calling you by name. Or while walking through a garden, imagine being strangely drawn towards a rhododendron bush that without warning bursts into flames and speaks. Yes, how dramatic. Unfortunately, these fantasies are not part of most people's real world. God speaks to real people who really want to hear through His Word, through prayer conversations, meditation, and of course, through His Church. God doesn't want to shout at His children (though to get their attention He sometimes needs to) but in the stillness.

A few years ago I entitled a worship album "In the Stillness," putting new music to the beautiful words written decades ago by E. May Grimes.

Speak Lord, in the stillness while I wait on Thee,
Hushed my heart to listen in expectancy.
Speak, O blessed Master in this quiet hour,
Let me see Your face, Lord, feel Your touch of power.
For the words You speak, Lord, they are life indeed,
Living bread from heaven now my spirit feed.
Satiate my being with Your fullness fill,
As the dew descending let Your speech distill.
All to You is yielded I am not my own,
Blissful glad surrender I am Yours alone.
Speak, Your servant hears now, be not silent, Lord,
Waits my soul upon You for the quickening word.
Fill me with the knowledge of Your glorious will,
All Your own good pleasure in Your child fulfill.
Like a watered garden, full of fragrance rare,
Lingering in Your presence let my life appear.

Two things before I continue. First, do you want to hear from God? Learn to linger in His presence. He does not share the secrets of His heart in hurried encounters. Second, do you feel that God has gone silent on you? Do you feel that He's not talking to you? My question to you is this: What was the last thing He said, and what did you do about it? *Whatever He says to you, do it.*

Many will understand when I say that so much of our lives and ministries are formed by those who are closest to us, our families. In the normality of every day experience, the interaction of loving lives, through the laughter and the tears, Jesus reveals Himself, His heart, His purposes and shapes us into the people that we are. Life's circumstances can either make us bitter or better. So much of my perspective of the Lord and therefore my approach to Him in worship has been birthed in me through such moments.

Lesley, my wife and I have five children. Rachel is studying medicine at Leicester University. All her eventful life (another story) she's been like a caffeine overdose! Active, against many odds, creative and noisy. Life is never dull!

Daniel, now nineteen, is like a valium overdose. He's so laid back he's almost horizontal!

Our triplets, now 14, are all different too. Mark Simeon is the eldest by fifteen minutes. Sport crazy in general, football in particular, he spends his days acting out seasonal sporting activities, hardly ever without a ball in his hand or at his feet. Sleep is a temporary inconvenience.

Sara Kate, is the youngest. She is 14 going on sixteen. She is addicted to talking!

Hannah Elizabeth, the second of the triplets, was born with a chromosome abnormality resulting in her requiring special education. She has neither Mark's mobility nor Sara's vocabulary. Bed time sees Mark celebrating in over the top fashion, in his imagination scoring the final winning goal. Sara talks to herself because she's run out of willing listeners.

Some years ago Hannah, with noise and confusion around, was used to climbing onto my knee for a cuddle. Her shape and mine matched. In the midst of the bedlam we were lost in each other's love. Her head buried in my chest, her breathing in unison with mine, life and time for a few precious moments, stood still.

"Daddy, I can hear your heart beating. Why?"

Moved by the simplicity and yet profoundness of the question, I replied, "Hannah, it's because you are as close to me now as it's possible for anyone to be."

The answer must have been sufficient. We soon slipped back into our "world without words."

We are obsessed with words, yet the Father's heart-beat is heard in that world that is beyond words. The throb of forgiveness, acceptance and affirmation is known in the pure intamacy between Father and child.

In a generation of broken marriages, single parents and child abuse the image of wholesome fatherhood is under siege. In truth, previous generations have had similar problems but they were veiled and hidden beneath the surface of respectability. Many times in counselling I've heard the cry, "I have no concept of a Heavenly Father... I cannot worship God as Father... I never knew a real Father." I've seen people almost choke on singing "Father in heaven, how we love You."

To those who have been so tormented and scarred, Satan will cause you to be obsessed by the scars, the loss, the pain, the injustice. Hell will always make the scars look ugly. *Heaven can make scars beautiful*. The scars of Calvary will be features of heaven that will be seen by the numberless gathering of the redeemed and will be revered and adored... By His wounds we are healed (Isaiah 53:5). Submit those scars to heavenly influences. Jesus can make all things beautiful.

Given that you are one of the many who feel robbed and cheated from enjoying a relationship with Father God because of the inadequacies of the human equiva-lent, may I ask, "What are you going to do now that you have no human role model of your Heavenly Father?" I'm not underestimating the heart ache, the regrets. The question though is still valid. Who do you look at to find out what your Heavenly Father is like?

...Jesus. If you've seen Him, you've seen the Father.

Turn your eyes upon Jesus. Learn from Him the joy of knowing the Father.

Doug Fowler

Doug Fowler has been involved in some form of music ministry for most of his life. At 13, he began playing guitar and leading worship for his high school chapel services. While attending Oral Roberts University, Doug had the opportunity to lead worship for a number of devotional and communion services. Then, as he was pursuing his career at Louisiana State University Medical School, Doug was called by the Lord into full-time music ministry. Serving under pastor Frank Bailey of Victory Fellowship in New Orleans for nearly seven years Doug helped build and establish the worship ministry of the church and recorded two live worship tapes.

In the following years, Doug served as music pastor for New Life Christian Fellowship in Jacksonville, Florida, and has also been instrumental in establishing worship teams, choirs and bands in a number of local churches through his Revival Fire Worship Weekends and Higher Call Ministries.

In addition, Doug helped found and coordinate the Jacksonville Alliance of Music Ministers (JAMM) with a mission of getting music ministers together for fellowship and city-wide gospel music events.

Doug has served as worship coordinator for Mario Murillo Ministries' crusades and is currently the worship leader for the "Catch The Spirit of Revival" crusades with evangelist Jesse Duplantis and Dr. Jerry Savelle. Doug and his wife, Susan, reside in Jacksonville, Florida, along with their three children. They are currently submitted to and ministering with Pastor J.D. Glass and New Beginnings, A World Outreach Center in Jacksonville.

The Heart Specialist

I am the oldest (and only son) of five kids born into the home of a medical doctor. By the eighth grade, I was studying Latin to prepare me for my journey to becoming a medical doctor myself. During this same time I was also teaching myself how to play guitar and taking some beginning piano lessons. Before I knew it, I was leading worship in my school chapel services in the mornings and dissecting worms and frogs in the lab in the afternoons.

Because my father was very active as a speaker in the Full Gospel Businessmen's Fellowship, my sisters and I were thrust into platform worship ministry at a very early age. With my mother's musical and costuming guidance, we would all dress alike (no dress for me, thank you) and line up like the Von Trapp Family Singers in front of thousands of people and sing such enduring classics as "Foolishness is Bound In The Heart Of A Child", and "So Do All Things Without Murmuring"! We didn't get any record deals, but the Lord used our small efforts to show thousands that a family who can worship together can certainly get God's attention.

I graduated from high school in 1978 and immediately enrolled in Oral Roberts University to pursue my Biology degree. Throughout my years as a student at ORU, I had several opportunities to lead worship in various settings such as dorm devotions or noon communion services. In 1981, I transferred to Louisiana State University in Shreveport to position myself for acceptance into the medical school there. While in Shreveport, God led me to plug into a growing new church there and get involved in the worship ministry. It seemed that at every turn I made in pursuit of my medical career, the Lord would position me into involving myself in a church music ministry to be trained and to train others.

Constantly, the Lord was imparting to me musical skills as well as enabling me to make very high grades in school.

Finally, in 1983, I fulfilled the first of my lifetime achievement goals. I was accepted into medical school in New Orleans, Louisiana. Now married, my wife and I were getting involved in another local church there in the New Orleans area. During the week I would be dissecting cadavers, observing autopsies, and reading endless volumes of medical textbooks. On the weekend I would play guitar, piano or tambourine in the church band, and would occasionally lead worship. I had a great balance going between the two very different lifestyles.

Then in June, 1985, in the middle of a 3-day fast, the Lord spoke to me and instructed me to withdraw from medical school and follow His call on my life in music ministry. Never had the thought entered my mind before that time. It was unheard of. What was dad gonna think? How would we make it financially? Everyone knows worship leaders get paid with "pats-on-the-back." So many questions, but God continued to ask, "Do you trust Me?"

So we stepped out in faith, believing God would supply all of our needs and He did. Nearly ten years later, we are still walking by faith for God to supply our needs and He continues to do so. What started out as a career in healing the physical man has turned into a career in healing the spiritual man. By gently leading people into His presence through worship, joy is found and strength is restored. The Word of God says, "A merry (or joyful) heart does good like a medicine" (Proverbs 17:22). God didn't take me out of the healing business. He just gave me a new prescription to give to others.

Trading Places

The secular philosophy in the corporate world is one of "Get all you can and can all you get." In our dog-eat-dog society, competition rules the work place. The fear of someone better than us taking our job can mar our performance and cloud our perspective.

My philosophy on this is radically different now, but it hasn't always been. Someone once told me that we as leaders should always be looking for, and training someone to take our place. Excuse me?!? Train someone to take my job?? No way!!

When I was first called into full-time ministry, things were exciting, fun and new. We added singers and musicians weekly to our fledgling program. Soon, it began to become bigger than I could handle on my own. So I began to pray for help.

One of the singers that had joined our team was a seventeen-year-old nervous-type, young man. He would constantly wear funky looking overalls, not only at rehearsals, but at church on the platform, too. He was never late, rarely absent and always joyful. Soon I began to notice that he would arrive early to help set up for rehearsals and to pray. Now I didn't hear an audible voice, or anything, but I felt impressed by the Lord to give this young man more responsibility in assisting me from week to week. All along, he would watch my every move, even to the extent of improving his singing voice on his own and teaching himself how to play the piano based on my style of playing.

I soon came to realize that God had answered my prayer. He didn't send me someone with a masters degree in music or a highly trained choir director. He sent me a servant. A young, funky-dressing servant ready to learn and self-motivated enough to pursue the level of excellence required for this kind of ministry.

Over the next several years this young man would become my closest assistant. He was my chief chair set-up man, my tenor section leader, my choir director, my volunteer secretary, and had even become my back-up worship leader. As he continued to gain more experience by leading worship at various youth and singles functions, God began to give him more and more favor with the senior pastor.

In 1990, God had spoken to me and my wife that it

was time for us to move on from there because He had something new for us to do. The next big challenge we had to deal with was who would replace me in leading a "cutting-edge" music ministry serving a congregation of over 2,500? For me the choice was obvious. Following numerous discussions with the senior pastor, it was decided that this young man would be part of a three-member team to help carry the music ministry through a time of transition. Finally, after serving faithfully as a volunteer for over 10 years under my ministry and as a part of the team, the Lord instructed the senior pastor to offer this young man a position as the full-time staff minister of music. I cannot express fully in words the joy I felt the day he called to tell me the news. Following years of sowing into his life, I finally saw the fruit of my ministry to this young man. God had given me the privilege of training the very individual destined to take my place. What a blessing.

So, if you are looking for an assistant, don't get caught in the trap of looking for the person with all the right paperwork. Remember, God chose a ruddy, young man named David to be king. He was a servant, a musician, and a shepherd. Someone with these qualities may be right under your nose!

Paul Baloche

Paul Baloche has become one of the most prolific praise and worship songwriters of our day, using musical styles relevant to today's generation and lyrics that come predominantly from the Bible or from his personal walk with the Lord. Over the past three years, as an exclusive songwriter for Integrity Music, Paul has written or co-written over 100 songs recorded by Hosanna! Music and others. His styles range from R&B, pop and rock to country and folk, enhanced by his background in acoustic and electric guitar.

As a worship leader, Paul's unpretentious and approachable style have encouraged many to draw near to God in worship. He has ministered throughout North America as well as several other countries. Paul travels leading believers in worshipful celebrations and conducting workshops on authentic worship, songwriting and musicianship. Paul is the worship leader on the Integrity's Hosanna! Music recording, "He Is Faithful."

*Presently he is serving as minister of music at
Community Christian Fellowship Church in Lindale, Texas.
Paul and his wife, Rita, reside with their three children in
Lindale.*

I Want to Be a 10-Talent Worship Leader

In my early twenties I attended Grove's School of
Music in Los Angeles, California. Grove was a one-year
trade school with a contemporary approach to harmony
and theory, designed to teach the skill necessary to
become a "working musician." While I was there I needed
to do a lot of studying and practicing, often working for
four or five hours a day at home on various things like
improvising, technique, arranging, etc. After awhile I
began to be concerned that I was being self-centered and
too focused on myself and my music. I struggled with
condemnation and guilt over the amount of time I was
putting into "myself." I thought that I should be praying
more, involved in some kind of ministry, and be more
outwardly focused. I also experienced these feelings after
we would spend many hours rehearsing with the praise
and worship team at our church.

This inner struggle went on for quite some time until one day, a heartfelt, honest prayer of mine to the Lord became a revelation to me. I prayed, "Lord, I just really want to play well enough so that I don't have to be preoccupied with what I'm doing musically. I want to be free musically to the point where I can focus on You and on the leading of Your Spirit and learn to `go with the flow' without being distracted by my lack of musicianship." It was one of those "ah-hah!" moments where nothing changed but everything changed! Although nothing had changed outwardly, I felt okay about my motives from that time on, because I knew that my heart was in the right place.

Little by little I began to realize that the investment of time I was putting into my musical education was an investment into the callings and gifts that God had given to me. The parable of the talents (Matthew 25:14-30) gives us a clear picture of God's attitude about how we invest · our talents and gifts.

In this parable Jesus talked about a man who, prior to going on a journey, entrusted his property to his servants. "To one he gave five talents of money, to another two talents, and to another one talent, each according to his ability." The story tells us that the servants receiving the five talents and the two talents each doubled the money for their master. The one-talent guy, however, "dug a hole in the ground and hid his master's money." When the master came back he was very pleased with the first two.

They had been faithful and he told them, "Well done, my good and faithful servant! You have been faithful with a few things; I will put you in charge of many things." But to the man who had buried his money the master said, "You wicked, lazy servant! So you knew that I harvest where I have not sown and gather where I have not scattered seed? Well then, you should have put my money on deposit with the bankers, so that when I returned I would have received it back with interest. Take the talent from him and give it to the one who has ten talents. For everyone who has will be given more, and he will have an abundance. Whoever does not have, even what he has will be taken from him. And throw that worthless servant outside, into the darkness, where there will be weeping and gnashing of teeth." Yikes! That's pretty heavy! (Selah!!)

I began to realize that a strategy of the enemy could be to keep God's people from pursuing excellence and keep them at a level of mediocrity. I believe Jesus was trying to tell us through the parable of the talents that God cares what we do with the gifts that He has put in us. There are many places in Scripture where God challenges and encourages us to pursue passionately our "callings," with an eye toward excellence.

I believe that we need to maintain our personal relationship with the Lord through quality time with Him developing a lifestyle of worship and prayer. As the Bible tells us to pray without ceasing, our times of practicing and rehearsing and playing can be continual offerings unto God. When we spend our time and energy perfecting our skills, we can work "as unto the Lord" so that He is able to use us in strategic places to influence others towards Christ and that we might hear those words one day, "Well done, my good and faithful servant."

Chuck Girard

Chuck Girard is one of the pioneers of contemporary Christian music and continues to be a voice of the move of God in that field.

Born and raised in southern California, Chuck began playing music at an early age, forming his first singing group in his early teens. The group, called "The Castells," hit the streets of Hollywood seeking success in the early '60s. They landed a recording contract that led to two national top-20 hits. This early experience led to a successful career as a studio singer and musician during the "surf" era of popular music. Eventually he became part of the "Hondells" and sang lead on their first two albums on Mercury Records. Their biggest hits were "A Younger Girl" and "Little Honda," the latter of which Chuck sang lead on.

Soon after this Chuck began to realize his need for God. He began a five-year search for spiritual reality through psychedelic drugs, Eastern religions and the like as he pur-

sued a "hippie" lifestyle in the '60s. This search ended in a then-small church in Orange County, California, called Calvary Chapel. Here Chuck found true spiritual reality through the gospel of Jesus Christ. After his new birth in 1970, he and four friends began ministry with the group "Love Song." The group became the first group to play rock-oriented music in the Christian setting and gain international acceptance and popularity in the early '70s revival know as the Jesus Movement.

After the disbanding of "Love Song" in 1974, Chuck continued to minister in a solo capacity, later that year releasing his first solo album featuring his most popular song, "Sometimes Alleluia." Over the years Chuck has released many solo albums as well as three with "Love Song."

His current album is called "Fire and Light," and recently he and his band-mates from "Love Song" got back together to record an album of fresh remakes of their early classics. The album is called "Welcome Back," on the Maranatha! label.

As well as continuing in his travelling ministry to the body of Christ, Chuck serves as an associate pastor and minister of music at Los Angeles Metrowest Christian Fellowship of West Los Angeles, California. Chuck currently resides in Chatsworth, California, with his wife, Karen, and their four daughters.

The Ways of the Spirit

Back in the earliest days of my own discovery of worship, I had an experience which impacted me so profoundly that I have never been the same.

I had just come through a time of correction in my life and was seeking God with a new sense of urgency. God had given me two mandates which became the guideposts of this period of my life.

First, He had said to grow up! I'd been a child of God long enough; it was time to become a *man* of God. Secondly, He said that if I was going to continue to characterize myself as a Christian musician, that I ought to see what *He* had to say about music. Hence an intense Bible study began that was to go on for some time, ultimately leading me into a discovery of worship from a Biblical perspective.

Around this time, there was a particular instance where I was seeking God in prayer. Even though I sensed His presence, there seemed to be no connection with His purpose in this time of prayer. I had been a Christian long enough at this time to know that this is a good time to sit down and listen. As I did, before long I heard the still small voice of the Lord say to me, "Would you go to the piano and play a concert just for Me?"

Unbelievable as it sounds, I had never done this before. I had started out in secular music for 10 years and had graduated immediately into the group, Love Song, as a Christian. Music was my "gig," and it never occurred to me to just sit down and worship. Significantly, God had invited me to give just Him a concert. This was to turn into probably the most profound worship experience of my life.

I began with a songbook that was on my piano, not having ever sung an entire worship song through from memory. Then I turned the page and saw a lyric that expressed something that I felt in my heart, but I could not play it because I did not know the melody. God prompted me to go ahead anyway, and He gave me a new melody for that lyric. Before long, I discarded the book and just began to sing freely to God, laughing and weeping almost at the same time.

This experience went on for some 90 minutes and was my first connection into the power of spontaneous worship. I didn't know the buzzwords then, such as "Song of the Lord," "Psalmistry," "The Secret Place," "The Inner Court," but all these things were happening in this tender learning experience. Since then, God has continued to teach me the "ways of the Spirit," and almost everything I learn to do in public comes out of my private times of worship as I seek God this way.

The Power of Silence

One of the things that I've always believed is that the maximum power of worship is not necessarily expressed in the more excitable type of celebration we often characterize as "good worship." This is not to say that we can't have a powerful experience that way, but as the Bible says in 1 Kings 19:8-12, "He wasn't in the wind; He wasn't in the fire; He wasn't in the earthquake, but in the still, small voice."

One time in the early days of what I was later to see was my personal revelation of worship, I had just finished a tape series on the value of edifying oneself by praying in the Spirit. On my way to a Sunday morning service not too far from where I live I decided to give this principle a trial run by praying in the Spirit all the way to the meeting, which was about a one and a half hour drive. About 10 minutes from my destination, I stopped and asked the Lord for a word for the church that morning.

Immediately I heard the voice of the Lord say to me, "When you get on the platform this morning, be absolutely silent for 15 minutes. I will do the rest." Well, this was not an easy word to receive as you can imagine. I was invited in as guest speaker/musician, and my reputation at that time was primarily for my musical gift. Silence was not what most were expecting that morning.

I immediately started what I jokingly call the "Abrahamic negotiations"! "Lord, would you bless for ten minutes of silence? Lord, what about even five minutes? that's still a long time." Then I went into some doctrinal tweaking, "Well, five minutes is a long time of silence. Perhaps God didn't mean a literal 15 minutes. Perhaps five will get the job done."

My sense of discomfort ruled over my sense of obedience for a time, and I had pretty well decided that I could get away with a meditative four or five minutes of silence and then sing some slow tunes to get into worship. But it was not to be. The second I set foot on the platform, as clearly as I've ever heard anything from the Lord, He said, "Well, you do what you want, but you know what I said!"

Dutifully, I faced the people and shared with them what I believed the Lord to be instructing. Quickly I took a seat on the piano bench facing the wall, head in hands, assuming a holy looking position, as I began to die a thousand deaths.

"I'll never get invited back here," I thought, as well as

the very spiritual, "There won't be much of an offering today!"

During the first five minutes, I could almost hear people thinking out loud, "What is this guy doing. I didn't come to church to be silent, I came to hear the Word," or any variation of an infinite amount of like comments. But...*after* the first five minutes, a hush settled in on the place, as the presence of God began to fill the room. You could sense the deep work of God as He pried into the parched hearts of many who probably hadn't taken five minutes to listen to God or bask in His presence in quite some time.

After the second five minutes, God began to impress me to walk into the crowd and deliver some words of knowledge. "God wants you to know that He has seen your pain, and He's not forsaken you. You've kept you heart right and God is about to bring deliverance." People began to weep as God touched their hearts with His comfort and love.

After I got back to the piano, I started to sing a couple of slow songs, working my way to some worship choruses as the people began to join in. The music built and crescendoed, and by the end of the service we were singing the victory songs and "rocking out"!

This was one of my most challenging experiences in trying to obey the voice of the Lord unconditionally. It is also my most profound experience even to the present time in seeing the power of silence in action.

Bob Fitts

To bring healing to the nations with the message of hope and encouragement in Jesus is the focus of the ministry of Bob Fitts. He has travelled to many parts of the world teaching, singing and worshipping with groups of people across denominational and cultural boundaries, drawing them deeper into love relationship with the Father.

Bob is a well-known songwriter and recording artist. He is the featured singer and worship leader on four of Integrity's Hosanna! Music albums: "The Lord Reigns," "Highest Place," "Bethlehem's Treasure" and "Proclaim His Power." He is also featured on Maranatha! Music's "Live Worship with Bob Fitts," and on two solo albums with Scripture and Song's Earth Mover division, "Take My Healing to the Nations" and "Sacrifice."

The many songs Bob has written include "Blessed Be the Lord God Almighty," "He Is Lovely" and "Let It Rain."

Bob has worked with Youth With A Mission in

Kailua-Kona, Hawaii, since 1981, where he pioneered the School of Worship at YWAM's University of the Nations. Bob and his wife, Kathy, and their four children reside in Kailua-Kona, Hawaii.

When Life Happens, Live It

If there is one message that is difficult to teach regarding worship, it is the message of *flexibility* and *humility.* Anyone involved in worship leading, or any public ministry for that matter, knows the challenge of developing these two very important character traits. Because heart issues are much more difficult to deal with than just passing on information, teaching them is often put on the back burner and replaced with some good strong head knowledge. It makes us feel better! We can then take an exam, be graded and have a form of evaluation put on ourselves and others. That would seem to be an alright thing to do—except that life comes along and happens! My wife and I have developed a saying, *"When life happens, live it."*

I remember a few years ago when a young boy

attending the youth ministry that I was leading wanted me to take him on a roller coaster ride. All of our group had traveled together to an amusement park (which specialized in roller coasters) and there we were, standing with our mouths wide open, looking up at this monster of a thrill ride. This young boy, whom I will call Bobby, kept saying, "Take me on it! Take me on it!" So after not too much persuasion, I got in line with Bobby and proceeded to enter the ride.

Now for those of you that have ridden roller coasters (however you feel about them), you realize that the moment you strap in, life begins to happen and there is a funny thing that goes on in your stomach (kind of the same feeling you get just before you lead worship for the first time). It is a mixture of fear and anticipation that for some is what the joy of living is all about—just enough challenge or danger to make your heart start pumping, and just enough safety so that you know nothing is really dangerous about it at all. It's almost an exercise in torture isn't it? Thrill rides are an effort to fool our senses into believing that we are really in danger. Sometimes our bodies (at least mine) take the bait. We are really scared!!

As Bobby and I embarked up that long hill, chain clicking, the sky looming before us as though we were heading straight into the clouds, Bobby looked me with the most horrified pale little face and said, "I want to get off!!" Oh I'm just sure!! As we went over the edge my leadership skills went into high gear. "Yo-o, ain't this fun?!" I said in a desperate attempt to salvage Bobby's confidence (worship leaders, pay attention, there are lots of parallels to note here!!!) No response, not even breathing, just terror. That hill finished, Bobby took a breath and with all his might screamed, "Get me off of this!!!"

How many times we've all felt like running off stage and dying. Just when you think it could never be worse... just ahead looms the next hill, more terror. By this time I was pretty upset that I had done such a stupid thing; however, by now the ride was almost over and things actually started getting fun. Bobby was gaining color and beginning to scream for joy. And then it began to happen, both mine and Bobby's perspective of the ride began to change. Thoughts like, "Boy, wait till I tell my friends about this ride," and "I meant to do that" were racing through our minds. After disembarking, little Bobby was right at me wanting to get on again! Ha! I was amazed. What a few minutes earlier seeming to be total disaster and danger, had now become one of the most memorable moments of my life (as is obvious by this very printing).

What did I learn? When life happens, live it. Hang on, my friend. What seems to be disaster is really all under control. You might say, "What on earth does this have to do with worship leading?" If you have done much leading or planning of meetings, you should quickly catch the parallels. Leading God's people to the place of praise and worship is one aspect of leadership that will always present an opportunity for real life to happen. How flexible and faithful we are in those situations determines not only how well people relate to us, but also how much all of us will enjoy experiencing the thrill of serving and honoring the Lord Jesus in praise and worship.

The latter of these two very important characteristics (and the one more obviously referred to in Scripture) is one I will relate in this next story. I remember once being asked to lead worship for a very large gathering of people. The praise team I was working with were incredible singers and musicians, most of them gifted worship leaders in their own right. As we were diligently rehearsing one day, I overheard one of the musicians comment about a young man who had written a song and wanted to present it in front of all these thousands of people. We were all a bit bothered by this, getting quite arrogant in sharing different horror stories of people who'd felt they needed to sing a song and were not ready for it (at least in our estimation). I could feel a bit of pride creeping into our rehearsal, and the Holy Spirit whispered to me, "Be careful." As I have led worship all over the world, I have come to recognize that voice as God's way of saying, "Don't put too much trust in your skill, in your gifting and talent; trust Me!" I told the team that God would probably humble us all and powerfully use the song.

Sure enough, that young boy was asked to get up in front of the conference and tell about a revival taking place on his high-school campus. After his testimony, he stood in great fear and trembling, but with a heart of humility and desire to honor God, and sang the song of praise the Holy Spirit had given him. He sang not so excellently, and the song (by songwriter criteria) was not so good, but God's Spirit loved the humble heart of his young servant and graced that auditorium with His wonderful presence. Here we were, these wonderful, educated, gifted people with loads of experience and knowledge to put our trust in, and God chose the young humble servant whose confidence was not in his gift, but in his God!!

Passing along to others the traits of flexibility and humility is not an easy task. Teaching life is difficult. We must do so by living it to its fullest. The Scriptures say: "Knowledge puffs up" (1 Corinthians 8:1). It's not often that we major on that concept in our schools of worship! I mean, aren't we there to teach people how to sing and play instruments and be good leaders? Doesn't God want us to have schools to teach people and to give them knowledge? Yes, but we also need a different kind of knowledge, the knowledge that God's ways are not our ways. We must learn the ways that get us outside our safe neat little environment and get us away from a rigid style that says "If you lead this song, they'll do that; if you say this phrase, this will happen; if you sing..." and so on. Certainly structure is important and a key component of any roller coaster. But in the analogy, getting on the ride means turning ultimate control over to the designer of the ride. Letting the Creator of life teach us through life's unexpected situations is sometimes the more difficult way of leading. Teaching structure is relatively easy, teaching lifestyle means we have to live it ourselves, walk it ourselves, "ride it" ourselves, even in front of those we lead.

Every praise service is God's moment to design a "new ride." As I have observed in retrospect just how much fun I get out of thinking about these kinds of situations, I find myself enjoying building roller coasters with tracks that go straight up the wall in seemingly disastrous configurations. God is not like that! He is good! He is the Author of abundant life!!

Steve Fry

Steven Fry is a well-known conference speaker and worship artist who brings a call for revival and passion for God to the forefront of his ministry. He is recognized as one of the leading writers of praise and worship music. Author of such well-known choruses as "Lift Up Your Heads" and "Oh the Glory of Your Presence," he has also penned two widely acclaimed musicals, "We Are Called" and "Thy Kingdom Come."

A wide range of involvements has served to enrich Steven's commitment to helping people discover the presence of God. For 10 years he pastored one of the largest youth groups on the West Coast. In 1983 he founded Messenger International, an association of pastors and local church leaders from around the country, which has mobilized over 10,000 young adults into short-term missions. His first book, a devotional entitled "Safe in the Father's Arms," was released in 1994. Steve has also just released a new album entitled "Fire in the Dark" and is in the final recording stages of a live praise tape to be released in the Spring of '95.

Steven and his wife, Nancy, live in Brentwood, Tennessee, with their three children.

God Inhabits Our Praises

For a number of years I had the privilege of leading high-school and college students in various outreaches around the world. On one occasion I was coordinating a group of about 200 young people in a street witnessing campaign in downtown Washington, DC. We had chosen a park in an area of the city which we later found out was one of the most violent in the entire District. So violent was this particular neighborhood that drivers could not stop their cars, and most certainly could not drive with unlocked doors for fear that their doors would be ripped open and they'd be robbed at knife point.

When we arrived at this particular park, we were confronted with a kaleidoscope of sights and sounds— pimps, prostitutes, and pushers, streetwise waifs and world-weary panhandlers. As we began to fan out through the park and surrounding neighborhoods sharing Christ's love with people, we soon realized that we were encountering forces of spiritual darkness that were beyond what we had encountered in the past. The atmosphere itself seemed to be charged with violence; some were becoming so belligerent that they accosted us within six inch of our faces, screaming obscenities. We knew that the situation could rapidly escalate beyond our control so we got some of the musicians together and began to play and sing praises to Jesus. Over the next several minutes we witnessed nothing short of a miraculous transformation. Suddenly a sense of peace and calm descended over the park. Where before onlookers were seething in their hatred, we now saw high school students sitting down and chatting amiably with scores of men and women about their eternal destiny. Later we found out that in the ensuing hour, 12 people gave their hearts to Christ!

What had made the difference? The difference was that the *authority of Jesus was brought to bear on that park through the praise and worship of His people*. Psalm 22:3, and we've quoted it often, says: "The Lord inhabits the praises of His people." A better translation is that the authority of the Lord is experientially realized in the context of praise. In other words, praise makes room for the Kingdom of Jesus to be established in a particular situation at a particular time. Never had Psalm 22:3 been made so real to me than on that day when I witnessed a bastion of violence transformed into an oasis of peace.

Heaven on Earth

Paul, the apostle, says in Ephesians 2:6 that we are seated with Christ in heavenly places. Paul's statement can be taken several ways. Is this a descriptive foretaste of what is to come? Is it Paul's way of poetically expressing our authority in Christ? Or does Paul's statement actually comment on present reality? After all, Paul is couching his words in the present tense. He says we are situated in a certain way at this very moment. We "are seated"—present tense—"in heavenly places in Christ Jesus."

How can this bear on a present reality that finds us fighting traffic jams and balancing check books? Actually there is something extraordinarily potent contained in this passage that "when we get a handle on it" will revolutionize our perspective and thus transform our lives.

The truth of this text was brought forcefully home to me some years ago when I was leading a group of college students in worship. We experienced an extraordinary encounter with the presence of God, and afterwards a college student, whom I had noticed sitting on the back row, came up to me with eyes as big as his face, his mouth gaping in awe. Knowing something of this young man's background, I knew he was an avid basketball player and had his Reebok's firmly planted on the gymnasium floor. He was not one given to mystical visions. Yet, here he was staring at me in semi-disbelief, describing to me what he had just seen while we were worshipping.

"While you were leading us in worship," he began recounting to me, "I saw two angelic beings on either side of you, so tall that I could not see beyond their shoulders. I looked straight up and as far as my eyes could see; I could still catch no more than their upper body. But the incredible thing was that behind you I saw the very feet of God." Now his encounter shouldn't surprise us because Scripture records in Exodus 24 that the elders under Moses also saw the feet of God from within the cloud of glory on Sinai. Had this young man seen a vision? I don't think so. I think for just a moment his eyes were opened to see where we actually live—in heavenly places!

You see, we're so used to thinking of heaven in directional terms, that it is a realm beyond the Universe. But heaven is not so much to be understood in directional terms—up, down, right or left—but in *dimensional terms*. Heaven is not another direction, but another dimension, coexisting quite literally with the material world. So in a very real sense, we are living in heaven now!

"Well, if that's true, it sure doesn't feel like heaven down here," someone might say. That is only because our perspective has not been altered. We are citizens of heaven expressing that life in the earthly realm. Though our eyes cannot see it, we are quite literally living in heavenly places *now* in Christ Jesus!

Yet someone might question, "What does this have to do with worship?" Everything! For if I realize that heaven is a dimension coexisting with the material world, then when I actually enter into worship I am actually joining the procession of the angelic hosts in lauding and adoring God. I am not attempting to coax God to come down here from heaven and manifest Himself as I worship Him. Through worship, I am tuning myself up to discover where I'm already living by the Spirit! This introduces a level of excitement and enthusiasm in worship that I would not otherwise know.

"But how," you might ask, "can I actually be joining heavenly worship in my finite locale? If God is truly omnipresent, how can His throne room really exist in my local church or my Bible study group?" Well that's one of the amazing things about God; He is so great He is not even limited by His omnipresence. For God is not only everywhere at the same time, He can localize His manifestations in an infinite number of ways simultaneously! That is the greatness of our God. Our passion to worship God will be great enhanced when we understand that when we worship we are quite literally joining the heavenly processional before the divine throne.

Geoff Bullock

Geoff Bullock spent his early childhood scaring the neighbors' cats and dogs with an assortment of loud, raucous instruments (piano, drums and guitar) before graduating to the pub scene... playing loud music to deaf drunks!

For nine years Geoff has been the full-time worship pastor at Hills Christian Life Centre in Castle Hill, New South Wales, Australia. During that time he has produced many contemporary praise and worship albums, including his own "The Heavens Shall Declare" and "People Just Like Us." The writer of more than 60 contemporary, popular choruses, his songs have been recorded by artists around the world.

Geoff has travelled extensively throughout Australia and New Zealand as a worship leader and seminar speaker. He was the worship leader at the Australian Christian Music Conference from 1988 to 1991 and has convened the Hillsong Conference since its inception in 1987. He is also the director for the new "Hillsong School," located at Hills Christian Centre.

Geoff and his wife, Janine, have five children and they reside in Sydney, Australia.

A Willing Heart

In May of 1988 I received a call from my pastor, Brian Houston. A renowned evangelist had canceled the second half of a crusade in the Philippines and Brian requested that I preach in his place. "Hey," I thought, "I'm a worship leader, a piano player, a songwriter, but an international evangelist?... are you sure you've dialed the right number?"

Three weeks later I found myself in a Philippine village and a strange culture with 150 fanatical filipino high-school students who were giving up their summer holidays to run crusades. I was hot, scared and feeling very much like a piano player not an evangelist. God...*help!!*

Early one morning we began our devotions. Me, 150 filipino teenagers, an out-of-tune 5-string guitar (with antique strings), a portable organ with a rhythm machine, and a collection of ancient choruses in various languages. The worship leader in me thought, "How can we worship God with this noise?!"

Five minutes later, however, nothing mattered as the Holy Spirit fell on us and we worshiped a God who favors a willing heart far above wonderful music.

I felt humbled. These people were wonderful musicians and singers. Their worship was pure and God-glorifying. Yes, it did sound a little strange, a little out of key, but God was listening more to their hearts than their music.

All of a sudden the evangelist in me realized God didn't want eloquence, He just wanted to use me.

That night the presence of God fell on us all as we witnessed hundreds of salvations. God desires a willing heart far more than a wonderful preacher.

Worship Live and Unplugged

"Just give me a microphone that works and a piano in the foldback" (that's "monitor" for you U.S. folks). I could hear my stressed voice filling the auditorium. It was 9:59 a.m. on a Sunday morning. The P.A wasn't working. The tech crew was running around chasing leads, microphones, fuses, musicians, singers, pastors... "Oh God, the congregation is looking at us with a look of expectancy on their faces. Just give me a microphone that works and a..." hold on a second... "Good Morning, Church!" I yelled. No microphone. No piano. I smiled at my panic and thought, "Who's in charge here?"

"Jesus," I prayed, "You said You would build your church and the gates of hell would not prevail against it."

I realized once again I had been side-tracked from the major issue. We started to sing. No microphone and no piano, but we did have a wonderful God who was on time, loves us heaps and wasn't deaf!! After the service we all prayed God would help us to be more prepared so that this would never happen again.

I prayed "God, please don't ever let me lose sight of why I'm here. If all else fails, You alone remain faithful and, therefore, nothing else need matter."

The next week we had a microphone, a piano, a full P.A. and a wonderful service. Above all we had the presence of God... just like the previous week!

David Butterbaugh

David Butterbaugh began leading worship shortly after he was saved in 1969. His worship leading experience began in "soul sessions," gatherings of young people singing Scripture choruses after evening church services. Searching for information about worship led David from one Christian bookstore to another only to find a lack of teaching material on the subject. Because of this, much of David's early worship leading was done by trial and error.

The elders at David's home church in Grand Rapids, Michigan, discerned an anointing on his life to lead the church body in worship during regular services. He did this for three years before moving to Dallas, Texas, to attend Christ for the Nations Institute. Graduating in 1980, David became part of the faculty at CFNI. He remained there for five years, leading the student body in worship and producing the annual worship tape, a project from which the Body of Christ has gleaned many popular songs such as, "Ah, Lord God,"

"As the Deer," "In Him We Live," "To Him Who Sits on the Throne" and many others.

In 1986, David became part of the pastoral staff of Word of Faith Family Church in Dallas, leading worship in local services, satellite seminars and on national television. During this time he was instrumental in helping with city-wide praise gatherings and the March for Jesus in the Dallas/Ft. Worth area. Since May, 1994, David has been ministering with Pastor Don Clowers at Grace Fellowship Family Church, a new church in the Dallas area. David was the worship leader on Integrity's Hosanna! Music's recording, "I Will Rejoice."

David and his wife, Beth, and their three children live in Coppell, Texas.

Manure Madness

"But the fruit of the Spirit is love, joy, peace, patience, kindness, goodness, faithfulness, gentleness and self-control. Against such things there is no law" (Galatians 5:22).

I was elected as a representative to the Student Council at a Bible school I attended several years ago.

The eight of us on that council used to meet every weekday morning to pray and discuss things that were taking place in the student life and the spiritual atmosphere of the school. Meeting on a daily basis gave us all plenty of opportunity to get to know each other and enjoy deeper relationships with each other. The frequency of our meeting also gave us the opportunity to irritate each other on occasion, as growing relationships sometimes do. It was during one of these irritating times in my own life that I sought the Lord earnestly on what to do about this, and my mind reflected on something I had not thought about in years. I saw this picture as clearly as if it were taking place at that moment, and the Lord used it to teach me a very valuable lesson.

When I was a young boy, our family lived on a farm in Dixon, Illinois, a small farming community in the north-central part of the state. My dad would plant crops, and raise livestock: pigs, cows, horses, and on occasion, sheep. We had a wonderful barn in which cows were milked, a hayloft to climb up into, and a separate shed with a large hay storage area and shelter for the animals.

I don't remember how frequently we had to undertake one particular chore, but it seemed all too often that dad would get out the Ford tractor with the front end loader on it and the old green manure spreader for the delightful job of cleaning up the barnyard. The hay and straw that got trampled underfoot mixed in well with all of the "natural" sediment that accumulated there. The job of cleaning the barnyard usually took the better part of a day and involved several trips to the field with the John Deere tractor spreading manure on the unplanted fields.

Down the gravel road to the lane we would go, sometimes freezing cold, sometimes dripping with perspiration from the heat. I always got nervous at this point, because I knew the responsibility that lay ahead of me. Once we traveled up the lane and arrived at the field of destination, my dad would step off the tractor and stand on the tongue (the part that hitched to the tractor) of the manure spreader. From there he would adjust the levers on the front of the machine that made the rotating barrels (located on the rear of the contraption) spin. One of the levers also controlled the speed at which the contents of the spreader were fed into these whirling barrels (which had long tines attached to them) to fling the manure high into the air and spread it out over quite an area of the field as we drove from one end of the field to the other.

My job at this point was always to sit on the seat of the tractor and steer our little train toward a fence post at the other end of the field. As we moved back and forth across the field, it seemed my dad would always wait until the last possible moment before jumping up on to the tractor to turn us around. I was always frightened that he would wait too long before helping me to turn around, and I just knew we would go crashing into fence posts and barbed wire and weeds along the fence row. Probably nobody would even come to look for us for days as we would be laying under our tractor/manure spreader (including its contents) wreckage! But father's wisdom always prevailed and we always made the turn before the on-coming disaster took place. Once the spreader was empty, off we would drive back to the barn to repeat this scenario all over again until the barnyard was entirely clean of all its contents.

But the worst thing about this particular task was not the cold or the heat. It was not the fear of the fence-crashing. It was the horrible smell of the "payload" we were spreading onto the fields! You just cannot imagine what would happen to my olfactory senses as we spread this horrid smelling stuff around the farm! As we drove across the fields with the manure spreader doing its job marvelously well, sometimes a big glob of this stuff would come slinging through the air and land on top of the tractor hood or, heaven forbid, even on my hat or in my lap! Ugh!!! I despised this job!

I used to look at those fields that we spread this stuff on and think that it was impossible for anything to ever grow in that soil again. I was certain that the smell alone would surely kill anything that even remotely resembled a crop! As time passed, the fields were plowed and disced and prepared for planting crops of corn, oats and hay. The seeds were inserted under the surface dirt and waited for rain and sunlight. During this time I would always wonder where the smell went, for all that I could ever detect with the spring planting season was nice, fresh, clean air and the odor of new blossoms on the neighboring trees and apple orchards.

After planting, I would sometimes ride my bicycle up the lane and look at those fields and I just knew that nothing would ever come up after putting that stinking "stuff" all over the field. But, lo and behold, the right conditions—a little rain, a little sun, and the right amount of time—always produced row upon row of green shoots as the oats and corn faithfully made their way up through the sod into the sun! I was always amazed that after a few months we would again travel to the fields with tractors and wagons, not to put anything into or on the field, but to harvest a great crop and put it into the corncrib or the hay loft for use during the coming winter.

At this point in my praying (remember, I am in Bible school when I remembered this story), the picture stopped and I found myself back on the steps in the student center, all alone with the Lord. I remembered the Scripture in Galatians that reveals to us what the fruit, the crop of the Spirit, is. Then I gently heard the Lord speak to me and declare that it was the manure, the fertilizer of adverse experiences in life, that will cause the fruit to blossom and grow and produce a beautiful crop in my life!

I cannot always control the situations I undergo in my life. However, I can sure allow the Holy Spirit to do His precious work, even though I sometimes think the situation "stinks," in order to allow Him to move and change my character and person to be more like Jesus.

Dan
Gardner

Rev. Dan Gardner is minister of music at Zion Evangelistic Temple in Clawson, Michigan. He has been on the full-time pastoral staff since 1980 and has a bachelor's degree in music from Oakland University. Dan's worship songs, published through Integrity's Hosanna! Music, are well-known internationally. Some of his most popular songs include, "My Life Is in You, Lord," "Blessed Be the Rock," and "Exalt the Lord Our God." Dan was the featured worship leader on Integrity's Hosanna! Music's "Praise and Honor" recording. Some of Dan's choral works, including "We Have Overcome," are published through Tempo Music.

Since 1981, Dan has ministered at worship/music conferences across the country, teaching on worship leading, song writing and other disciplines. His heart to see Christian musicians raised up to be a powerful influence both within and outside the church has led Dan to begin the Christian Musicians Network, the purpose of which is to train and equip musicians for ministry.

Dan, his wife, Joanne, and their two daughters live in Troy, Michigan.

Simple Praise, Simple Solution

Nearly every time I share about the subject of worship I tell about a personal encounter with the Lord that profoundly changed my personal worship and helped shape my underlying motivation for leading God's people in praise. This lesson came to me about 12 years ago through my daughter, Angela, when she was a vibrant three-year-old toddler.

Wednesday afternoons have been my prayer and preparation time for leading worship in our mid-week service for over 17 years. Typically, as on this day, I sat at the piano in my living room to prepare for the evening service. This particular afternoon, I was struggling to come up with the all important "Worship List." I had prayed and spent time worshipping the Lord, reading the Word and doing everything I would normally do to prepare—yet I was still coming up empty. Not a single song. As the clock kept moving forward I began to sweat. 3:00. 4:00. 5:00. The clock kept ticking but still nothing.

Becoming increasingly desperate, I started fumbling through my alphabetical song list to grab those songs that have worked in the past, or maybe, just maybe, the Lord would impress me with the right songs as I gazed at their titles.

I scanned through my 300-song list at least two or three times. Nothing! I looked through worship lists from past services. Nothing! I was dry. I have never enjoyed these "dry" spells (though they certainly teach one trust and reliance upon the Lord, don't they?). As far as I knew, there was no unconfessed sin to stand in the way. I was desperately trying to do my part by seeking God, truly wanting to get His heart for this worship service. This seemed much more overwhelming than it needed to be!

Frustrated and growing more anxious, I left the piano to go into the kitchen to get something to eat (my carnal reaction to stress). The kitchen in our home is adjacent to our family room. I was drawn away from the refrigerator and stepped toward the family room. As I walked to the edge of the room, an overwhelming sense of God's presence met me at the door.

As God's presence flooded my heart, I peered into the family room and noticed my three-year-old daughter, Angela, kneeling on our couch, looking out the picture window toward the heavens. Her eyes were fixed on something outside the window and her hands were raised high. Angela was singing ever so quietly in her sweet little voice, "I love you Jesus; I praise you Jesus."

Tears flooded my eyes as I watched her pouring out her heart of love to the Master. In those moments, I enjoyed what I had been yearning for all afternoon. I had been just two rooms away!

I have never forgotten that experience. When I find myself striving and sweating to get into worship, this experience reminds me that the motivation for my personal worship and ministry is this: *I must allow the love that Christ deposited in my heart to flow back to Him in a nonpretentious, simple way.* As I rested in that love on that Wednesday night and many services since, I have found Him to be faithful to meet us.

Author Listing

Daniel Amstutz
917 Hedin Circle
Anaheim Hills, CA 92807
714-281-4824 HM
714-535-1961 CH

Paul Baloche
303 Lakeview Dr.
Lindale, TX 75771
903-882-8502
903-882-5675 FAX

David Baroni
Bethel Chapel
P.O. Box 51
Brentwood, TN 37024
615-371-1000

Stephanie Boosahda
Inner Court Ministries
2911 NW 122nd St — Ste 222
Oklahoma City, OK 73120
405-751-4742
 or 751-0550

LaMar Boschman
P.O. Box 130
Bedford, TX 76095
817-540-1826
817-540-9608 FAX

Chris Bowater
Lifestyle Ministries
113 Yarborough Crescent
Lincoln LN1 3NE
ENGLAND
011-44-52-254-1570 (0860)

Rev. Clayton Brasington
5555 N. Federal Hwy.
Ft. Lauderdale, FL 33308
305-771-8840

Geoff Bullock
Hills Christian Life Centre
P.O. Box 1195
Castle Hill NSW 2154
AUSTRALIA
011-61-2-634-7633
011-61-2-899-4591 FAX

David Butterbaugh
252 Heather Glen
Coppell, TX 75019
214-393-2173 HM
214-401-1967 CH

Morris Chapman
120 South Jones Blvd
Las Vegas, NV 89107
702-878-0615

John Chisum
c/o Integrity Music
1000 Cody Rd.
Mobile, AL 36695
334-633-9000

Kim Clement
P.O. Box 293303
Lewisville, TX 75029-3303
817-491-0090

Don Dalton
2206 South Abbey Loop
New Braunfels, TX 78130
210-606-1962 HM
210-620-5433 CH

Danny Daniels
13740 E. Quincy
Aurora, CO 80015
303-420-4793
303-456-8865 FAX

Lynn DeShazo
P.O. Box 43097
Birmingham, AL 35243
205-969-2831

Brian Doerksen
Pacific Worship School
5708 Glover Rd.
Langley, BC V3A 4H8
CANADA
604-530-8463

Eddie Espinosa
P.O. Box 18329
Anaheim, CA 92807
714-777-4777

Bob Fitts
YWAM
76-6256 Koko Olua Place
Kailua-Kona, HI 96740
808-334-0147
808-326-2343 FAX

Doug Fowler
Higher Call Ministries
P.O. Box 51332
Jacksonville Beach, FL 32240
904-223-5099
904-223-9979 FAX

Steve Fry
Messenger Fellowship
P.O. Box 474
Brentwood, TN 37024-0474
615-370-1322
615-370-1323 FAX

Dan Gardner
Zion Evangelistic Temple
3668 Livernois
Troy, MI 48083
810-524-2400

David and Dale Garratt
Scripture in Song
P.O. Box 28-741
Remuera Auckland 1005
NEW ZEALAND
011-649-523-1802
011-649-523-1804

Chuck Girard
P.O. Box 33226
Granada Hills, CA 91394-0026<%0>
818-882-7908
818-882-1625 FAX

Eugene Greco
His Banner Ministries
P.O. Box 142
W. Milford, NJ 07480
201-853-8532 PH & FAX

Michael Green
Faith Church
13123 I-10 Service Rd.
New Orleans, LA 70128
504-241-1234

David Grothe
Victory Christian Center
7700 S. Lewis
Tulsa, OK 74136
918-488-1980
918-493-3492 FAX

Gerrit Gustafson
Kingdom of Priests
P.O. Box 850311
Mobile, AL 36685
334-661-9777
334-660-1154 FAX

Vivien Hibbert
Shady Grove Church
1829 W. Shady grove Rd.
Grand Prairie, TX 75050
214-790-0800

Ray Hughes
9626 Cainsville Rd.
Lebanon, TN 37090
615-286-2758

Steve Ingram
P.O. Box 10261
Daytona Beach, FL 32120
904-322-0020
904-322-0097 FAX

Dennis Jernigan
P.O. Box 890358
Oklahoma City, OK 73189
918-472-7475
800-877-0406
918-472-7479 FAX

Kevin Jonas
Christ For the Nations
P.O. Box 769000
Dallas, TX 75376-9000
214-376-1711 EXT. 6502

Bob Kauflin
Abundant Life
Community Church
5104 N. I-85 Access Rd. —
Suite 3
Charlotte, NC 28206
704-596-4994

Graham Kendrick
Make Way Music
P.O. Box 263
Croydon CR9 5AP
ENGLAND
011-44-81-656-0025
011-44-81-656-4342 FAX

Tom Kraeuter
Training Resources
8929 Old LeMay Ferry Rd.
Hillsboro, MO 63050
314-789-4522
314-789-5735 FAX

Steve Kuban
Crossroads Cathedral
4745 Highway 7
Woodbridge, ONT L4L 1S6
CANADA
905-851-8086

David Lawrence
Piano-By-Ear and
Gospel Arts Institute
P.O. Box 47099
Atlanta, GA 30362
800-44-BY-EAR Nationwide
404-391-0606 in Atlanta
404-263-6064 FAX

Bob Mason
The North Church
1615 West Belt Line Road
Carrollton, TX 75006
214-242-8989
214-245-1978 FAX

Don McMinn
2322 Creekside Circle South
Irving, TX 75063
214-432-8596

Len Mink
10600 Sprucewood Lane
Cincinnati, OH 45241
513-777-0949 PH & FAX

David Morris
Springs Harvest
Fellowship
1015 Garden of the Gods
Road
Colorado Springs, CO 80907
719-548-8226

Howard Rachinski
CCLI
6130 NE 78th Ct.
Suite C11
Portland, OR 97218
503-257-2230
800-234-2446

Joel Ragains
3600 Kamer-Miller Rd.
New Albany, IN 47150
812-944-6448

Jeanne Rogers
P.O. Box 222
Hurst, TX 76053
817-267-4211

David Ruis
c/o Metro Vineyard
Fellowship
11610 Grandview Rd.
Kansas City, MO 64137
816-765-2822

Tim Smith
20885 SW Deline
Aloha, OR 97007
503-848-7664

David Wright
The Living Word
6927 Lefferson Rd
Middletown OH 45044
513-424-7150
513-424-7822 FAX

John Wyatt
2131 W. Ina Rd.
Tucson, AZ 85741
520-297-7238

Equipping
THE
Church
FOR
Worship

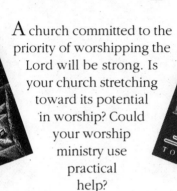

A church committed to the priority of worshipping the Lord will be strong. Is your church stretching toward its potential in worship? Could your worship ministry use practical help?

"In very practical, down-to-earth terms Tom leads you through a journey into the heart of the effective worship leader... a journey needed by us all! While he writes from a praise and worship background I could find little that could not be used by any church music leader of any denomination."

Bill Rayborn
The Church Music Report

"Tom Kraeuter has special insights into practical apllications of worship/music teams, their development and on-going well-being. His experience will aid the building and growth of church praise and worship departments."

Kent Henry
worship leader on five
Hosanna! Music recordings

Keys to Becoming an Effective Worship Leader
or
Developing an Effective Worship Ministry
Either book just $7.95 each!

Both books also now available on audio cassette!
The complete text of either book on two tapes, read by the author.
Just $10.00 for either book on audio tape!

Training Resources Order Form

TITLE / DESCRIPTION	PRODUCT #	QTY	PRICE	TOTAL
			Subtotal	
			Shipping/Handling	

US/Canada, add 10% on $0-$50. Over $50, add $5.00 only. For foreign orders
(outside US/Can) add 40% to all orders for air shipment, 15% for surface shipment.

TOTAL

PAYMENT OPTIONS
(check one)

❏ Enclosed is my check or money order for $_____ in US currency.
(Make checks payable to Training Resources.)

❏ Credit Card
Please bill my: ❏ **MC**   ❏ **VISA**   Credit Card Expiration Date:_____

Card#_____

Cardholder's Signature_____

Name_____

Address_____

City_____State_____Zip_____Country_____

Mail to: Training Resources • 8929 Old LeMay Ferry Rd. • Hillsboro, MO 63050
Please include street address as UPS does not deliver to P.O. boxes.
Please allow 4 - 6 weeks for delivery.
☎ Telephone orders (charge cards only) call: (314) 789-4522, ☎
Monday through Friday, 8:30 - 4:30 CST.